Beyond Happy

Women, Work,
and Well-Being

BETH CABRERA

atd
PRESS

Author's Note: The names of some of the people portrayed in this book have been changed.

ATD Press is an internationally renowned source of insightful and practical information on talent development, workplace learning, and professional development.

ATD Press
1640 King Street
Alexandria, VA 22314 USA

Ordering information: Books published by ATD Press can be purchased by visiting ATD's website at www.td.org/books or by calling 800.628.2783 or 703.683.8100.

Library of Congress Control Number: 2015945447

ISBN-10: 1-56286-979-5
ISBN-13: 978-1-56286-979-3
e-ISBN: 978-1-60728-305-8

ATD Press Editorial Staff
Director: Kristine Luecker
Manager: Christian Green
Community of Practice Manager, Human Capital: Ann Parker
Developmental Editor: Kathryn Stafford
Text Design: Maggie Hyde
Cover Design: Julia Prymak, Pryme Design
Printed by United Graphics LLC, Mattoon, IL, www.unitedgraphicsinc.com

Contents

Contents

Acknowledgments

· ·

I OWE MUCH GRATITUDE to the many wonderful people who helped transform this book from a dream into reality. Thank you wholeheartedly to my generous friends, all busy with your own work and families, for taking the time to read early versions of this book. This includes Susan Godfrey; Jen McCabe; Amy Lucchesi; Amy's mom, Suzanne Haskell; Lisa Nason; and Susan Minarik. I am especially grateful to Debbie Haverstick, Karyn Mallett, and Tami Moffitt, for your feedback, and to Paula Tarnapol Whitacre, for your gifted editing. All of your insights and suggestions made this a much better book.

I also thank those of you who told me your stories and trusted me to share them. My appreciation goes out to the Alumni Office at Thunderbird for allowing me to survey your women graduates. A sincere thanks to the hundreds of women who took the time to respond to my survey and to those of you who were willing to spend even more time sharing your personal experiences with me in follow-up interviews. Thank you, Allison O'Kelly and Caroline Evans at Mom Corps, for letting me survey your members. I am grateful to the many women who chose to participate.

To the great team at ATD Press, it has been a privilege to work with you. Thank you, Ann Parker, for believing in this book and for your patience and kindness throughout the publishing process. Thanks to my editor, Kathryn Stafford, for your expert guidance and understanding.

I'm grateful to my colleagues at George Mason University's Center for the Advancement of Well-Being for all you have taught me and for inviting me to be a part of such an exciting endeavor. A special thanks to Nance Lucas and Todd Kashdan for your support and advice. To my friend and mentor Steve Gladis, who was confident that I could write this book and offered me valuable advice each step of the way, a huge thank you. I'm fortunate to have had numerous other colleagues provide me with opportunities and guidance throughout my career. Thank you all.

I am forever grateful for my parents, Mary Lynn and Keith Fraser, whose love and belief in me have been a constant source of support throughout my life. My awesome sister, Katherine Fraser, encouraged me from the beginning to write this book and gave me thoughtful suggestions and feedback along the way.

Above all, I thank my husband and our amazing children for the joy and meaning they bring to my life. Ángel, I am so blessed to be on this journey with you. Thank you from my heart for your love and support, for reading countless excerpts from the book, for sharing your wisdom, and for giving me the confidence to try new things. To Alex and Emily, thank you for cheering me on, putting up with me when I obsessed over the book, and making my experience as a mother more wonderful than I ever imagined it could be.

Introduction: Struggling
to Manage It All

· ·

Like most mornings, Lynn heads to the gym after dropping her kids off at school. As she runs on the treadmill, she makes plans for the day. Last night her daughter said she had to bring snacks for her soccer team tomorrow. When will Lynn find time to get to the store? Her son told her on the way to school he wants to try out for the play. Her mind races as she worries about adding another after-school activity to their already packed schedule.

Lynn checks her email on the way to the car. Her 9:30 meeting has been pushed up to 9; she better hurry! As she drives to work, she frets about not having time to prepare the presentation she is giving in a couple of days. She feels her stress level rising while waiting at a traffic light; will she make it to the meeting in time? She just makes it, then spends the rest of the morning trying to work on her presentation, but with a constant flow of emails to respond to she makes little progress. She eats lunch at her desk so she can keep working. Her friend Ann sends an email asking if she wants to go out to dinner with a group of friends next week. Wouldn't that be nice? But just thinking about all she'd have to do to make it work stresses Lynn out, so she sends a quick response to Ann, "Maybe next time." The afternoon is spent tackling one problem after another. Lynn has no energy and feels as though she is facing an endless series of meaningless tasks. She sneaks out early to run by the store for the soccer snacks before picking up the kids from their after-school program.

When she gets home, Lynn responds to emails as she makes dinner and talks to the kids about their day. Her husband, Jeff, rushes in as she is putting the food on the table. They start the dinner conversation arguing about who is going to get the snacks to the soccer field tomorrow. Then Jeff announces a business trip has just come up. Great! Lynn checks her email once more before going to bed; her boss has called a morning meeting to discuss a problem with one of her biggest accounts. Despite feeling utterly exhausted, she has trouble falling asleep because she is now worried about tomorrow's meeting and juggling the family's schedule.

Does any of this sound familiar? Women have made huge strides during the last several decades to achieve greater equality in education and in the workplace. But we certainly haven't figured out how to have it all. In fact, striving to have it all is pushing more and more women to the breaking point.

In her book *Overwhelmed: Work, Love, and Play When No One Has the Time*, Brigid Schulte describes the intense time pressure that women are experiencing. Rising levels of role overload lead to a feeling of never having enough time to attend to a never-ending list of responsibilities. Constantly switching from one role to another "splinters the experience of time into thousands of little pieces," which intensifies the feeling of overwhelm.[1]

This may explain why women's level of happiness has declined over the past 40 years, both relative to where they were and relative to men.[2] According to the American Psychological Association, 28 percent of women report having a great deal of stress versus 20 percent of men. Forty-nine percent of women versus 39 percent of men say their stress level has increased during the past five years.

Significantly more women than men report physical and emotional symptoms of stress such as headaches or upset stomachs.[3] A 2014 survey by Care.com found that 80 percent of working mothers feel stressed about getting everything done.[4]

As a working mother, I suffered from the stress of trying to do it all. I loved my job as a college professor and I loved being a mother, but I didn't love the person I had become. I spent my days complaining to my colleagues. I yelled at my kids and then felt guilty. And I knew my husband was tired of listening to my constant stream of "poor me." I wasn't even able to enjoy spending time with family or friends over the weekend because I was so stressed about all I felt I should be doing. The generally happy, upbeat person I used to be was gone.

My frustration led me to start doing research on women's careers. I quickly discovered that I wasn't alone. The struggle to combine our role at work with our essential role at home is negatively affecting women's well-being. We continue to face gender discrimination along with unrealistic expectations and a lack of support. Neither societal norms nor work models have kept up with our evolving roles. Thus began my search for solutions that could help us all live better lives.

I surveyed and interviewed hundreds of women to gain insight into the strategies they were using to manage it all. Further research led me to the work being done in positive psychology, which, as I explain further in chapter 2, is the science of what leads to thriving in individuals, workplaces, and communities. Topics studied include hope, optimism, love, resilience, strengths, flow, purpose, and meaning.

I began applying some of the concepts I was learning to my own life. As I became more mindful, I worried less. I started focusing on what was going well in my life instead of dwelling on problems. I used my values as a guide when deciding how to spend my time. I looked for ways to make a positive impact on people around me. As a result, my well-being improved.

Well-being is a subjective sense of how our lives are going. Achieving well-being was a concern of philosophers as far back as Aristotle, yet interest in the topic has grown significantly in recent years. A great deal of research is currently being done on the factors that both influence and constitute well-being. Countries are starting to include measures of well-being as indicators of national progress and success. Cities like Santa Monica, California,[5] are adopting strategies for improving the well-being of people in their communities as part of an effort to create meaningful social change.

In my quest to improve women's lives, I have spent the last several years studying well-being. The multiple factors that influence our well-being can be categorized into two main dimensions: feeling good and doing good. The first dimension is how we feel on a day-to-day basis. People who experience more frequent positive emotions have higher well-being than those who feel good less often. The second dimension of well-being is how we evaluate our lives overall. People who sense their lives are worthwhile because they are pursuing meaningful goals and making a positive difference have higher well-being than those who don't feel they are doing good.

The workplace is changing, and so are societal norms. Women's lives will get better as a result. But change isn't happening fast enough. Women want to be thriving now.

My goal in writing this book is to suggest some practical solutions for improving women's well-being. Combining the results of my research on women's careers with findings from positive psychology, I offer advice to women who are eager to experience greater well-being right now.

The book is divided into four parts. In part 1 (chapters 1 and 2), I lay out the factors that contribute to women's struggles and suggest avenues for improvement. I then present a two-dimensional model of well-being and provide a self-assessment exercise that can be completed to determine your current level of well-being. The results identify areas to focus on as you work to boost your well-being in order to thrive. Specific strategies are listed at the end of each chapter.

Part 2 (chapters 3 through 5) focuses on the first dimension of well-being: feeling good. I describe three strategies—being mindful, being grateful, and being hopeful—which can help you feel good by experiencing more frequent positive emotions. Part 3 (chapters 6 through 8) addresses the second dimension of well-being: doing good. Three ways to increase your sense that your life matters because you are doing good are to live your values, develop your strengths, and make a positive impact.

In part 4 (chapters 9 and 10), I explain that relationships are the most important factor for well-being because they contribute to both the feeling-good and the doing-good dimensions of well-being. I discuss the importance of connecting with others and offer suggestions for how you can strengthen your relationships. Four strategies for building high-quality connections are to engage in positive interactions, show appreciation, establish trust, and be generous.

Throughout the book, I present the most relevant positive psychology research, along with practical pieces of advice that you can start applying today to transform your life. I have included anecdotes from my own life, as well as stories from women I know and others I interviewed for my research. I am confident that within these pages you will find ideas to help you manage the turmoil and create a life of greater joy and meaning. My hope is that you find the book to be as enjoyable as it is useful.

Part 1

The Path to Well-Being

· ·

"Being a woman is hard work."
—Maya Angelou

THIS SECTION ADDRESSES THE issues that are negatively affecting women's well-being, as well as the factors that
contribute to well-being. Chapter 1 discusses the difficulties that women are experiencing. Outdated workplace policies and
structures make it extremely difficult for us to fulfill our multiple
roles. Stubborn societal norms of men as breadwinners and women
as caregivers prevent us from getting the support we need. Continued gender discrimination makes the situation even worse.

Chapter 2 offers a way forward, presenting a model of well-
being that can be used to identify strategies that women can adopt
to increase their well-being. There is a self-assessment exercise that

you can complete in order to determine your current level of overall well-being. The assessment also provides a sub-score for each of the two dimensions of well-being: feeling good and doing good. The results of the assessment provide a road map that you can follow to start making changes in order to create a more joyful, meaningful life.

1

Women and Work

. . . .

*"Most of us have trouble juggling. The
woman who says she doesn't is someone
whom I admire but have never met."*
—Barbara Walters

HOW HAVE WE REACHED this point in the first place? This
chapter addresses the challenges women face at work, in
addition to the issues we are dealing with at home.

What's the Problem?

Women face numerous obstacles as they struggle to advance their
careers and to have full, happy lives. A major factor contributing to
the pressure that women are under today is the difficulty of trying
to perform so many different roles. Add to all of this the increased
societal pressure to look and feel like a million bucks, and it's not
surprising that women are unhappy. Trying to successfully fulfill
so many roles at once is impossible! And that's not all. Women still
face gender discrimination at home and at work, which further
increases the amount of stress and frustration that we experience.

Difficulties Combining Work and Life

A great deal of the stress that women experience is due to the unique challenges they face combining work with life. Many aspects of the workplace have remained virtually unchanged over the past 100 years. Changes in societal norms have also lagged behind the evolving role of women. Because of this, women experience a significant amount of work-life conflict, which often leads to stress and unhappiness.

The world of work has not kept up with the changing workforce. In 1950, 63 percent of the households in the United States were made up of a male breadwinner who worked outside the home and a female caregiver who stayed home with the children. Today, only 17 percent of households follow this traditional model.[1]

Yet work is still organized around the traditional "ideal" worker, a man who is able to dedicate himself completely to his job because he has a wife at home taking care of the children and the household. Face time at work and perceived sacrifice continue to be used to judge an employee's performance and commitment, regardless of whether or not these contribute to results. The problem with these norms is that they work against women who have multiple roles to fulfill.

These traditional policies work against men, too. In fact, the workplace is even less friendly to fathers who want to spend time with their children and be an equal partner at home. Men are stigmatized for going against the breadwinner norm, often being punished more harshly than women. Requesting parental leave or flexibility in many cases can lead to lower performance ratings, fewer promotions, and smaller raises.[2] Until workplace structures, policies, and cultures adapt to meet the needs of modern families, women and men will continue to struggle with the issue of work-life conflict.

Women want meaningful careers that offer them the flexibility to be mothers at the same time. Those who aren't mothers also need more freedom to choose when, where, and how to work. Women are far more likely to take responsibility for the care of aging parents than men. Daughters spend an average of 12.3 hours per month caring for their elderly parents compared to 5.6 hours for sons.[3]

The extreme hours and relentless travel that are often requirements for success in many jobs make it impossible for women to perform their various roles. Men often can't help because they put their jobs at risk if they ask for flexibility. This leaves women feeling pressured to choose between work and family.

Many women who are financially able to do so end up opting out of their careers.[4] Samantha Nelson is a good example. She was making a six-figure salary as an account director of a large global advertising agency. She had a demanding job and a long commute. When her two children started becoming involved in after-school activities, she decided it was time to quit her job.

> *I wanted the full-out career, same as a guy, with all the responsibility and the money and the bonuses and perks, and I wanted all the benefits of being a mom and a joyous life and all that stuff. It's not possible. I needed to have more flexibility. When I was at work I felt like I should be home, and when I was home, I felt like I should be at work. And I had had quite a career by that time. I didn't feel like I could be the kind of mom I wanted to be and keep my job. You can't truly delegate it all. Motherhood can't be outsourced. That is not the way I wanted to do it.*

Living in a society that undervalues the role of caregiving doesn't help the situation. The United States is one of only four countries that has no national law mandating paid family leave.

The other three countries are Lesotho, Papua New Guinea, and Swaziland. Child care is often unaffordable or undependable, and about half of Americans get no paid sick time at all. I was fortunate to be working in Spain when both of my children were born and after each pregnancy I had 16 weeks of fully paid maternity leave. We also had access to affordable child care. These were both critical factors in my decision to continue working after my children were born.

In 1990, the United States had one of the highest rates of employment for women in the world. However, a lack of family-friendly policies has contributed to a decline from a peak of 74 percent of women in the workforce in 1999 to only 69 percent today. Many other countries have adopted policies aimed at keeping women employed, such as generous parental leave, subsidized child care, and part-time work. As a result, the following countries now have a higher percentage of women between the ages of 25 and 54 working than the United States: Sweden, Norway, Switzerland, Denmark, Germany, Canada, France, Britain, Portugal, and Japan.[5]

Trying to combine work and family becomes even more stressful when women feel pressure to do it all. The feminist movement fought hard to give women more choices. The goal was to free them from their limited roles as housewives and mothers. It sought to give them greater opportunities by breaking down barriers in a male-dominated society. The movement was successful in giving women greater access to education and employment. However, society's expectation that women carry the bulk of the responsibility for housework and child care has not changed.

Women today have more options than they have ever had, but rather than recognize that having choices means you can choose among them, women feel like they need to do everything, to have it all. Trying to be the perfect spouse, the perfect mother, and have the perfect career leaves women feeling as though they aren't measuring up.

Increased demands at work and at home make it even harder to measure up. Work hours are becoming more and more extreme. For many employees, the 40-hour work week is a thing of the past. In 2009, married middle-income parents worked about eight and a half hours more per week than in 1979.[6] A study of high-earning professionals showed that 62 percent work more than 50 hours a week, 35 percent work more than 60 hours a week, and 10 percent work more than 80 hours a week.[7]

In addition to more extreme work hours, standards for mothering have also increased. In 1975, mothers who worked outside the home spent an average of six hours a week on primary child care compared to 11 hours for stay-at-home mothers. Today, mothers employed outside the home spend 11 hours per week on primary child care versus 17 hours for stay-at-home mothers.[8] So, working mothers today are spending the same amount of time with their children as stay-at-home mothers did in the past.

Not only are mothers spending more time with their children, they are doing far more for them than ever before. The ideal mother is expected to provide stimulating activities for her children, plan extravagant birthday parties, shuttle her kids from sports practices to music lessons to after-school tutoring, and, of course, have a healthy, home-cooked dinner on the table every night.

As long as we equate the ideal worker and the ideal mother with 24/7 availability, women will have to make choices and making choices requires trade-offs. Different women make different choices. Yet whatever choice we make, we often wonder whether or not it was the right one. Will my children resent the fact that I was always working? Would I have made partner by now had I not requested a reduced schedule after my maternity leave? Worrying about the trade-offs we have to make contributes to the stress and unhappiness that women experience as we try to combine work and life.

Gender Discrimination

Despite significant advances, women still face discrimination in the workplace. And while overt discrimination is becoming less prevalent, subtle but real biases are still quite pervasive. These subtle forms of discrimination can be just as detrimental to women's careers as more traditional, overt discrimination.[9] This puts women at a disadvantage at work, which leads to additional stress and frustration.

Joan Williams has studied women and work for over 25 years. She is the director of the Center for WorkLife Law at the University of California Hastings College of the Law. Through her research she has identified different types of gender bias that women encounter. She and her daughter, Rachel Dempsey, describe these biases and give women advice on how to handle them in their book, *What Works for Women at Work: Four Patterns Working Women Need to Know*.

First, they found women have to prove themselves over and over again. This occurs because women are judged on their *performance*, whereas men are more often judged on their *potential*. People notice men's successes more than their mistakes, whereas they notice women's mistakes more than their successes. Furthermore, men's successes are attributed to skill, while women's successes are attributed to luck. The opposite is true for failures. This means that men, much more so than women, are given the benefit of the doubt when they make a mistake. Williams and Dempsey found these biases come about due to the stereotypes many people hold regarding women and professionals. Assumptions about successful professionals align with masculine rather than feminine stereotypes.

Second, because of these stereotypes, women are held to a double standard. They are expected to behave in traditionally feminine ways, yet masculine behaviors are required to be successful at work. Women who are "too feminine" are judged to be low on competence, while women who are "too masculine" are judged as not being nice; likability is expected of women. This means women have to work to maintain a precarious balance, combining competence with likability.

Third, they found further discrimination results from the strong negative assumptions that associate motherhood with a lack of competence and commitment. Mothers are often not offered promotions or challenging assignments due to these assumptions. A job applicant who is a mother is 44 percent less likely to be hired than a woman without children.[10] Maternity leave and flexible or reduced-hours schedules simply exacerbate the potential for discrimination. So the pressure to prove themselves over again becomes even greater when women become mothers. It turns out that even women who are not mothers can suffer from this bias because most people assume they will have children at some point.

Cindy Lawrence encountered blatant discrimination at two different companies. She was working in the international division of a bank in Chicago when her first child was born. Her husband was relocated to Minneapolis around the same time, so Cindy quit her job. She had planned to look for a part-time job once they got settled, but when she tried to find a day-care center there weren't any good options, so she decided to stay home.

Eight years later, Cindy and her husband divorced, and she went back to work. Here is what she told me:

> I remember distinctly an interview I had with a
> major international insurance firm. I was on the third
> interview, and I thought for sure I had the job. They were
> talking about their training program and introducing

me around. I didn't say anything about being divorced. I just said, "Hey, my youngest child is in preschool; I have been waiting for this moment. I'm so ready to go back to work." The guy that was the head of the office turned around and said, "So, just how many children do you have?" When I said three I knew I should have lied. I saw this look cross his face. They ended up hiring someone else.

Another woman at a bank I ended up working for asked me directly, "What are you going to do when your kids get sick? I don't think you can do this job." What was I going to say? "You could be fired for asking me that question." But I wanted the job.

Rebecca Nelson also shared her frustrations with me. As marketing director for an international publishing company in Dallas, she handled all of the marketing of the books for their U.S. clients and was responsible for about a million dollars in sales each year. Rebecca loved her job until her first child was born. She explains how things derailed quickly:

My boss decided that I shouldn't travel because I had a young child. I wanted to travel and didn't think in any way that my having a child should impact my work. I thought it was unfair. The other problem was that most of the people in the office were young and single. They would go out for drinks after work and talk about work and make decisions without involving me. Then I hired a young guy and found out that he was getting all the projects that I should have been getting. At that point, I just decided that I had had enough. My husband got a job offer in Atlanta, and he wasn't going to take it. But I found out this other guy in the office was getting

*a really big project, so I quit, and we moved. I was
very angry!*

A fourth challenge that Williams and Dempsey identify is that
gender bias can lead to conflict among women. As women make
difficult decisions about how to handle the problems facing them at
work and at home, tensions may arise when they judge each other
based on what each one personally believes is the best strategy.
Women from different generations have adopted diverse strategies
to deal with their unique experiences. The so-called "mommy wars"
pit women with children against those without, as well as mothers
against each other, based on what each believes is the right way to
mother. At times, women worry whether or not they are making
the right choice. These deeply personal decisions can cause women
to be defensive and critical of each other rather than supportive.

Gender discrimination is not only frustrating for women, but
it also contributes in part to the wage gap between them and men.
The fact that women in the United States are paid only 78 cents
for every dollar that men are paid[11] hurts many families. Around
40 percent of mothers are primary breadwinners, and another 23
percent are co-breadwinners.[12] All of these families are economical-
ly disadvantaged as a result of the gender wage gap.

The wage gap can negatively impact women's well-being by
increasing the amount of financial stress they experience. In one
survey, 28 percent of women reported high levels of stress due to
money issues, compared to 17 percent of men. Of those who said
they were experiencing "overwhelming financial stress," 9 percent
were women and 3 percent were men.[13]

In addition to gender discrimination at work, women face
gender discrimination at home. We are still socialized to believe
that men should be the breadwinners and women should be the
caregivers. In families where both the mother and the father work
full time, women do an average of 28 hours of housework a week

compared to 16 hours for men. Mothers spend about twice as much time caring for children as fathers do.[14] The fact that women still shoulder the brunt of responsibilities at home brings us right back where we started: the issue of work-family conflict that causes such stress in women's lives.

Given the lack of support that women receive as they attempt to fulfill both work and nonwork responsibilities, the gender discrimination they continue to face, and the pressure to not only do it all, but also do it all perfectly, it's no wonder that women's well-being is declining.

Fortunately, there are signs that things are changing. A heightened awareness of subtle gender biases is helping to reduce discrimination in the workplace, where employee policies are slowly becoming more flexible. These changes will eventually result in a greater number of female leaders in organizations. Women in leadership roles will advocate for new, more flexible ways of working, and gender discrimination will become less prevalent. There seems to be a tipping point where discrimination decreases when women make up at least 25 percent of a group.[15]

Men are also starting to push for change. Younger generations are more interested in having lives outside of work and want to be equal partners when it comes to child care and housework. According to a study by the Families and Work Institute, 75 percent of Millennials, who are between the ages of 18 and 35, don't expect to have partnerships that follow traditional gender norms.[16] As these men begin to take on more and more of the responsibilities at home, women will experience less work-life conflict and will be more likely to seek higher levels of responsibility at work. Men will also need more flexibility, so they, too, will advocate for new ways of working.

The problem is that change is not coming fast enough. For years, companies believed in the "pipeline" theory; if they hired enough women at entry-level positions, more and more women would rise to the tops of companies over time because there would be a larger pool of female candidates for leadership positions. Well, it turns out that there is a major leak in the pipeline.

For 20 years now, almost half of graduating physicians, lawyers, and PhDs have been women. Half of all workers in the United States are female. Yet, a 2012 McKinsey survey of 60 major corporations showed that 325,000 women had entry-level positions, 150,000 were middle managers, and only 7,000 had made it to vice president, senior vice president, or CEO.[17] The number of women in leadership roles seems to be stuck at around 16 percent. Women represent 16 percent of major law firm partners, 18 percent of Congress, 14 percent of Fortune 500 CEOs, and 15 percent of corporate board members.[18]

What Can Be Done?

Until significant advances occur in the workplace, in government policies, and in society, women need knowledge and practices that will empower them to reduce their stress, increase their resilience, experience more joy, and find more meaning in their lives.

I have spent the last 18 years trying to find solutions for managing my own life as a working mother. I met and married my husband while we were both graduate students at Georgia Tech in Atlanta, where I was studying industrial/organizational psychology. We received our PhDs in 1995 and moved to my husband's hometown of Madrid, Spain. I had started learning Spanish while we were dating and was still struggling to speak the language when we moved. The university where I was hired as a tenure-track professor, Universidad Carlos III de Madrid, allowed me to teach my management class in English during the first semester while I worked to improve my Spanish. By the time the second semester rolled around I was teaching in Spanish, ready or not.

I was actually pretty popular. The students would bring their friends to sit in on my classes because I was so entertaining. My rudimentary knowledge of Spanish led me to say all sorts of things; some were funny, and some were apparently quite inappropriate. As my Spanish improved, I was able to spend less time stressing about teaching and more time focusing on doing the research I needed to do in order to get tenure.

In the meantime, our son and our daughter were born. After each birth I took the government-mandated four-month maternity leave and then returned to work. We were blessed to have a fantastic nanny, Carmen, who gave me enormous peace of mind every morning when I headed out the door. We were also lucky that my parents-in-law lived in Madrid, and they were happy to help out when we needed them.

I knew Carmen was taking great care of the kids, but I wanted to spend as much time with them as I could. So I made a point to leave the office every afternoon around five, which is early in Spain, where people typically work until at least seven or eight. I remember wondering, as I walked past the doors of all of the male professors still working, how I could ever keep up. How much longer would it take me to publish enough articles to get tenure if I left at five every day?

I spent fewer hours in the office but managed my time carefully. The hard work paid off, and I eventually did get tenure, a few weeks after our daughter turned two. I was elated! I was the first American to earn tenure at the university. It was a critical milestone in my academic career, and I was proud of myself for having achieved it in a different culture and a foreign language.

Less than three years later, my husband was offered a job as president of the Thunderbird School of Global Management in Arizona. As much as I loved living in Spain, I was excited about the opportunity for our children to experience life in the United States, and I recognized that it was a great career move for my husband. So I walked away from my hard-earned position.

I then had to decide what to do with my career. Our children were five and seven years old. We left our nanny and my parents-in-law behind in Madrid. My husband's job involved attending numerous institution and community events, many of which I was also expected to attend. And I had other responsibilities as first lady, such as organizing events for the spouses of the Thunderbird board members when they met several times a year and giving presentations to various groups. Given my current situation, I didn't see any way I could try to earn tenure again.

I considered opting out of my career. An article entitled "The Opt-Out Revolution," in the *New York Times Magazine*, caught my eye. Author Lisa Belkin had interviewed a group of women who had graduated from Princeton; some had also earned law degrees from Harvard and Columbia. They had worked as lawyers, managers, and journalists. But when Belkin spoke with them, almost all of them had left their careers to stay home with their children. The only one who was working full time had no children. Maybe it was time for me to follow suit and opt out.

One night my husband and I got a babysitter and went out for a date night. Over dinner at a nice restaurant, I started sharing my thoughts with him about not looking for a teaching position but instead staying home with the children. At some point, I couldn't even finish what I was saying. People at the other tables started to look over at me.

I realized then how much I enjoyed teaching and how difficult it would be to give it up. Knowing that a full-time faculty position was not a good option for me at that point in my life, I decided to take a part-time position at Arizona State University. It didn't have the distinction of my prior position, but it allowed me to continue doing a job I loved on terms that made it possible for me to also fulfill my many other responsibilities.

That's when I started doing research on women's careers. My own personal experience got me thinking about just how hard it is to be a woman today. I felt called to use my training as a scientist to try to find solutions for women who are struggling. After surveying 500 women graduates of Thunderbird, many of whom were pursuing careers in international business,[19] I followed up with interviews to hear more of their stories,[20] then surveyed over 600 more women who were exploring flexible work options through a professional staffing company.[21]

Almost half of the women I studied had quit their jobs at some point. I asked them why. Their answers were diverse, but almost always involved some variation of stress caused by work-life conflict or frustration associated with gender discrimination in the workplace.[22] I realized that what many researchers were focusing on—how women could find balance—was not addressing the fundamental issue. Advice from self-help books on how women could have it all wasn't the solution either. Let's face it; these are both impossible goals. The real concern for women is not finding perfect balance or figuring out how to have it all. What women want, what we all want, is to lead joyful, meaningful lives.

I later decided to leave the university and start my own business—working directly with women and the companies that employ them to promote positive change. In addition, I wanted to make sure that I wouldn't have to give up my career when we moved again for my husband's next job. Some of the women I interviewed for my research had mentioned the advantages of having a "transportable career" if you were part of a dual-career family.

I know firsthand the challenges of combining motherhood with a professional career. I have experienced the difficulties of being part of a dual-career couple. There are a lot of tough choices to make and day-to-day stresses to deal with. As I learned about positive psychology and discovered interventions through my research, I started applying them in my own life. As a result, I have become happier and less stressed. My relationships have improved, and I feel that my life has more meaning. I want to share what I've learned so that you, too, can benefit. That's why I wrote this book.

Women can't wait for government policies to provide them with the support they desperately need. They have to be proactive and take steps to improve their lives right now.

My hope is that by reading this book you will learn strategies that will help you engage in meaningful change in order to live your best life. There is no one-size-fits-all formula. Each of us has our own unique life with different values and ever-evolving circumstances. We have to make our own choices. But I have identified some key elements that can help everyone be happier and more fulfilled despite daily challenges.

You can thrive at work and in life by focusing on having what matters most for your well-being. Our well-being is enhanced when we experience frequent positive emotions—that is, we feel good—and when we sense that our life has meaning—that we are making a difference by doing good. We experience more positive emotions when we are mindful, grateful, and hopeful. Our lives are infused with a greater sense of meaning when we live our values, develop our strengths, and make a positive impact on others. Strong, supportive relationships contribute to both our happiness and our sense of meaning. Let's explore how.

2

Understanding Well-Being

* *

"Well-being cannot exist just in your own head. Well-being is a combination of feeling good as well as actually having meaning, good relationships, and accomplishment."

—Martin Seligman

I N 1998, WHEN HE was president of the American Psychological Association, Martin Seligman challenged psychologists to broaden their primary focus on human problems to include more research on what promotes flourishing. This kicked off the positive psychology movement, which studies what leads to thriving in individuals, workplaces, and communities. At the individual level, researchers have been working to determine what affects our well-being.

Many different factors contribute to our well-being. Carol Ryff, a researcher at the University of Wisconsin, includes six components in her measure of psychological well-being: autonomy, self-acceptance, purpose in life, environmental mastery or feeling in control, positive relationships, and personal growth.[1] Another group of researchers, Joseph Ciarrochi, Todd

Kashdan, and Russ Harris, identify seven foundations of well-being: functional beliefs such as having hope and self-esteem, mindfulness and awareness, perspective taking or empathy, knowing your values or purpose, experiential acceptance rather than trying to avoid or suppress your thoughts and feelings, behavioral control like willpower and resilience, and cognitive skills that help you solve problems and adapt.[2] According to Seligman, five essential elements are required for well-being: positive emotion, engagement, positive relationships, meaning, and accomplishment or achievement.[3]

There is a good deal of overlap among these different theories of well-being. In looking at the many factors that determine our sense of how our lives are going, most of them can be categorized into one of two dimensions:

1. "Feeling good"—our experience of positive emotions or happiness

2. "Doing good"—our sense of meaning in life; the feeling that what we are doing matters.

Figure 2-1 shows how these two dimensions contribute to well-being. People who are high on the feeling-good dimension experience more frequent positive emotions. They are happy, joyful. People who are high on the doing-good dimension have a sense of meaning in life because they feel they are making progress toward valued goals and are making a difference in the lives of others. In order to thrive, we need to be high on both dimensions, experiencing both happiness and a sense of meaning in life. People who are low on both dimensions are languishing.

FIGURE 2-1: DIMENSIONS OF WELL-BEING

High	Happy Life	Thriving
Feeling Good		
Low	Languishing	Meaningful Life

Doing Good

Many researchers agree that well-being is about more than just being happy. In *Authentic Happiness: Using the New Positive Psychology to Realize Your Potential for Lasting Fulfillment*, Seligman distinguishes between pleasures and gratifications. Pleasures create positive emotions, while gratifications come from using your strengths and aligning your behavior with your values. Gratifications require skill and effort. They can lead to the absence of emotions, like when you are in a state of flow, or may even lead to negative emotions such as frustration or anxiety. He believes both pleasures and gratifications are important for well-being. In his book *Flourish: A Visionary New Understanding of Happiness and Well-being*, Seligman reiterates that positive psychology is about more than happiness. Positive emotions are one element of well-being, but well-being is about more than just feeling good. It also comes from using our strengths in the pursuit of meaningful activities that fully engage us. It is about doing well over time.

In a similar way, author Jennifer Hecht makes a distinction between good-day happiness and good-life happiness, explaining that good-day happiness is associated with positive emotions that can fluctuate on a daily basis, while good-life happiness comes from engaging in tasks that give our lives meaning.[4] She concludes that positive emotions contribute to our well-being, but that we also need obstacles and challenges for our lives to have meaning.

Nobel Prize winner Daniel Kahneman contrasts happiness, a current mood, with life satisfaction, which is our emotional reaction when we think about our lives. He explains that buying a new car may increase our happiness, while our life satisfaction has more to do with our life goals and whether or not we are achieving them.[5] According to Kahneman, "a definition of subjective well-being that ignores people's goals is not tenable. On the other hand, an exclusive focus on satisfaction is not tenable either. If two people are equally satisfied (or unsatisfied) with their lives but one of them is almost always smiling happily and the other is mostly miserable, will we ignore that in assessing their well-being?"[6]

Think for a moment about your own well-being. Into which of the four regions of the chart do you fall? Are you happy? Does your life have meaning?

Feeling Good

Why is feeling good so important for our well-being? It turns out that positive emotions provide us with a number of benefits. For one, they help people build valuable psychological resources. Positive people have better mental health, experiencing less anxiety and lower levels of depression. They are also more hopeful, self-confident, and resilient.[7] People who are hopeful and self-confident set higher goals, generate multiple pathways for meeting their goals, and expend a good deal of effort in order to reach their goals. Positive people are more resilient because they have more effective coping skills. They are proactive and problem focused when facing obstacles. They are able to bounce back from setbacks, not letting difficulties deter them from pursuing their goals.

Positive individuals tend to have stronger relationships. People feel closer and more connected to others when they experience positive emotions. This makes them more likely to make favorable judgments of people, which increases liking and leads to closer relationships. Strong relationships are critical for thriving because they serve to further increase positive emotions and also give us a sense that our lives are meaningful.

Positive emotions can lead to greater creativity and better decision making because our emotions affect the way our minds work. When we are in a negative mood, our minds have a very narrow focus. This can be useful in helping us to respond rapidly to an imminent threat. When we hear a honking horn, it is in our best interest to ignore everything else and look for the car to see if we are in danger. When a customer calls with a complaint, we should listen carefully and focus on trying to resolve the situation.

When we experience positive emotions our minds work in the exact opposite way. Rather than narrowing our focus, the range of ideas and behaviors that come to mind when we are in a positive mood are much broader.[8] Positive people are more mindful of what is going on around them; they take in more information. This leads them to make better decisions because they are more open and see more solutions to problems. Also, when people experience positive emotions they feel safe and secure, so they can think in more divergent ways without feeling threatened. Thinking outside the box leads to greater creativity.

Alice Isen, a psychologist at Cornell University, and her colleagues were interested in the influence of positive affect on decision making. In one study they asked third-year medical students to decide which of six hypothetical patients most likely had lung cancer. To induce a positive mood, some of the medical students were given a bag of candy beforehand. Being in a positive mood led students to be more open to examining all of the different pieces of information available to them. As a result, the students who received the candy were nearly twice as fast in making the correct diagnosis and exhibited much more creativity than those who didn't receive candy.[9]

Positive people are also physically healthier. They have lower blood pressure, lower heart rate, lower levels of stress-related hormones, and stronger immune systems. Positivity lowers the probability of hypertension, diabetes, and stroke. Positive people sleep better, have fewer colds, and report experiencing less pain than negative people.[10] And thanks to these health benefits, it is estimated that positive people may live up to 10 years longer than negative people.[11]

Feeling good is a key dimension of well-being due to the many benefits of experiencing positive emotions. So you may be curious as to whether or not you can control the amount of positive emotions you experience. It is true that some people are naturally more positive than others. The belief that a good portion of our happiness is due to genetics comes from a study of twins carried out by David Lykken and his colleagues at the University of Minnesota. They collected data about the happiness of hundreds of pairs of identical and fraternal twins. Some of the twins had been raised together in the same household, but others had been raised apart. Their results showed that identical twins had very similar happiness levels, even those who had been raised in different families. On the other hand, the correlation between the happiness scores of fraternal twins was close to zero. These findings provide convincing evidence that perhaps as much as 50 percent of our positivity is due to our genetic make-up.[12]

While this means that we all have a set point for our happiness that is determined genetically, it doesn't mean that we can't do anything to increase our positivity. Our set point only determines about half of our happiness. So what about the other half? Many people think that life circumstances play an important role in our positivity. They would be surprised to find out that our circumstances actually have a very small impact on our happiness.

Studies have shown that wealth, education, your physical appearance, where you live, even your health are all barely correlated with happiness. American income has increased significantly over the last 50 years, but life satisfaction has remained the same. The happiness boost that people report after plastic surgery doesn't last.[13]

Life circumstances have such a small impact on our positivity because human beings adapt rapidly to new situations. Our brains are wired to respond to novelty, so we readily notice what is new and different and tend to ignore what becomes redundant in our lives. New life circumstances, like moving to a city with a much better climate or getting a promotion, may temporarily increase your positivity, but when the novelty wears off, so, too, will the effect on your happiness.

In order to study the effects of adaptation on happiness, researchers from Northwestern University and the University of Massachusetts compared the happiness level of a group of major lottery winners to a control group. They also looked at the difference in happiness between a group of paralyzed accident victims and a control group. The researchers found that the lottery winners were no happier a year later than were average individuals. They also discovered that, after adjusting to their new life, paralysis victims were only slightly less happy than average individuals.[14] The process of adapting to change can clearly be helpful when bad things happen in our lives.

So genetics accounts for about half of our positivity, establishing a set point that we naturally move toward unless we do something to change it. We could try to change our life circumstances, but that will only have a small, temporary impact on our happiness, because we rapidly adapt to any new situation. What, then, determines the rest of our happiness? It turns out that the amount of positivity that we experience is due in large part to our thoughts and actions. This means that we can intentionally choose to think and act in ways that will increase the amount of positive emotions we experience.

It does require a conscious effort, however, because our brains are wired to focus on what is bad rather than what is good. We are constantly on the lookout for potential danger. We pay more attention to negative events and react to them more strongly. We typically remember four negative memories for every positive one.[15] We also feel negative emotions more intensely than positive emotions. Rick Hanson, a neuropsychologist who writes about how we can change our brains to experience greater happiness, has a great way of describing our negativity bias. According to Hanson, "the brain is like Velcro for negative experiences, but Teflon for positive ones."[16]

This negativity bias played an important role in keeping our ancestors alive, but in the modern world, where being attacked by a saber-toothed tiger is much less likely, paying so much attention to negativity is not as crucial as it was in the past. Yet our innate tendency to focus on problems or perceived threats causes many people today to suffer from chronic stress. Women, who are trying to juggle so many different roles and responsibilities, have an especially high risk for experiencing stress.

When we experience stress, our bodies generate chemicals that are harmful to us. Chronic stress can lead to headaches, gastrointestinal and cardiovascular problems, diabetes, hormonal imbalances, and a weaker immune system. Stress also contributes to skin conditions, asthma, and arthritis. Other health problems related to stress include anxiety, depression, and alcohol or drug abuse. Chronic stress can even cause the prefrontal cortex, the part of the brain responsible for higher-order thinking and decision making, to deteriorate.[17]

Our well-being depends on our ability to counteract this natural propensity to focus on the negative. Staying positive requires considerable sustained effort to keep our attention focused on the right things. Obviously, we can't avoid negativity in our lives; bad things do happen. What matters is the ratio of positive-to-negative emotions over time. Because of our negativity bias, we need more positive emotions to outweigh the stronger negative ones.

The good news is that we have the power to improve the ratio of positive-to-negative emotions. We can do it by changing the focus of our attention. Most of the stress we experience is the result of our thoughts. Situations don't cause stress. Our brains cause our stress. William James, who is considered by many to be the father of American psychology, said, "the greatest weapon against stress is our ability to choose one thought over another." We can learn skills to change our thinking style. And what I find to be even more fascinating is that we can actually change our brains by changing the way we think.

Research in neuroscience has found that our brains are rewired in response to our thoughts and emotions. What we pay attention to changes the structure and function of our brains. The technical word for this is *neuroplasticity.* Hanson explains that our attention is "like a combination spotlight and a vacuum cleaner: it illuminates what it rests upon and then sucks it into your brain."[18] If our minds spend most of the time focused on anger, worry, or self-criticism, our brains will come to naturally focus on similar things. Likewise, the more our minds focus on joy, serenity, or self-confidence, the more our brains will notice good things.

When we focus on something, specific neurons fire together in our brains. The more often neurons fire together, the more likely they are to fire together in the future because the neural connections become stronger. Have you ever noticed that no matter how many walkways there might be in a park, people always seem to find a more direct route across the grass? After enough people walk the same way over and over again the grass gets beaten down, and a path is formed. The same thing happens in our brains. By intentionally directing our attention in the same way over time, we will create a new path by changing the neural connections in our brains. This means that we have the power to rewire our brains so that we experience less stress and are more positive, resilient, productive, and happy. It is possible to increase the feeling-good dimension of our well-being by choosing thoughts and actions that lead to more frequent positive emotions.

Doing Good

Being happy or feeling good is necessary for our well-being, but it isn't sufficient. People who are thriving also have a sense of satisfaction with their lives because they feel their lives have meaning. They believe what they are doing is valuable and worthwhile.

Like happiness, meaning in life is related to many positive outcomes, including higher self-esteem, less anxiety, greater use of effective coping skills, lower levels of depression, and better health.[19] The positive impact that meaning in life has on health led a group of scientists at Rush University in Chicago to investigate whether or not meaningfulness is related to life expectancy. They asked 1,238 people in their seventies about their sense of purpose in life and followed up with them five years later. The researchers concluded that people with a higher sense of meaning in life have a 57 percent lower risk of mortality than people with a lower sense of meaning.[20]

Roy Baumeister is a psychologist at Florida State University who studies meaning. He has concluded that, while there are factors that contribute to both happiness and a meaningful life, there are also some key differences between the two. Happiness or feeling good is more self-focused. It is about getting what we want or need in the present moment. Meaningfulness or doing good is more about effort, giving, and sacrifice. It involves integrating the past, present, and future in a meaningful way. It is related to doing things that express oneself, as well as doing positive things for others. Involvement in meaningful activities can actually reduce happiness by increasing stress and anxiety.[21]

According to Baumeister, people have four needs that must be satisfied in order to experience meaning in their lives. The first need is for purpose or to have a life aim. Having a goal for the future gives people a sense of meaning. Working toward an objective is a valuable pursuit. The second need is for values. Values help people decide how to act and provide them with a sense that they are doing the right thing. A feeling of self-efficacy is the third need. This is the belief that a person has control over his or her life and can choose to make a difference. The final need is for self-worth. People experience increased levels of meaning when they believe they are good or worthy.[22]

Michael Steger directs the Laboratory for the Study of Meaning and Quality of Life at Colorado State University. He believes meaning in life involves two elements: comprehension and purpose. Comprehension is our need to make sense of or see significance in our lives. It is about understanding one's self and how we fit into this world. Purpose is our need to do. It is about striving to accomplish an overarching set of objectives. People who understand who they are and why they are here and who are invested in important life-long goals experience a greater sense of meaning in life.[23]

So our sense of meaning or doing good comes from pursuing goals that matter to us personally, as well as pursuing goals that matter to others. Goals are personally or intrinsically satisfying when they let us be authentic by expressing our true self. Goals matter to others when achieving them makes a positive impact in someone else's life. Three ways, then, to increase the doing-good dimension of well-being are to live your values, develop your strengths, both of which contribute to an authentic life, and make a positive impact by serving others.

Engaging in activities that are consistent with our own values and beliefs lets us feel authentic because we can be ourselves while performing them. Kennon Sheldon at the University of Missouri has spent much of his career studying personal goals, in particular, the impact of personal goals on well-being. According to his model of self-concordance, behavior that is consistent with one's values and goals leads to higher levels of well-being.[24]

We live our values when we align our actions with what we believe to be right or good. We feel we are doing good when we have a clear sense of what we believe is important and we make decisions based on those beliefs. Many of us have a life purpose that comes from our values. Our purpose guides us to consistently choose goals that are congruent with our values, which helps us to feel satisfied with our lives.

A second way to do good by living authentically is to develop our strengths. Strengths are built when we invest in our natural talents. This requires that we become aware of our talents, practice using them, and acquire skills and knowledge that help us refine them. Using our strengths is energizing. We perform at our best when we pursue goals that allow us to use our unique combination of talents. Developing our strengths contributes to our life satisfaction because it leads to a sense of competence and efficacy. It gives us a sense of meaning to feel that we are realizing our potential.

A third strategy for increasing meaning in life is to pursue goals that make a positive impact in the lives of others. The feeling that we are making the world a better place or putting "a ding in the universe," as Steve Jobs said,[25] gives us a sense that we are living life in a fulfilling, satisfying way. Serving the greater good by actively engaging in pursuits that transcend our own immediate interests can give us immense satisfaction. It lets us see the significance of our lives. Putting aside our selfish interests to serve others gives us a sense of purpose and helps us feel valued.

In some cases, doing good can also make us feel good. We often experience positive emotions when we are using our strengths. And it feels good to make a decision that is aligned with our values. But doing good doesn't always make us feel good in the moment. As Baumeister suggested, it can, in fact, lead to negative emotions. We will face setbacks as we pursue our goals, which can lead to frustration. Doubt about whether or not we will achieve our goals can lead to anxiety and stress. There may be conflict with people who stand in our way or try to persuade us to follow another path. But experiencing these difficulties is often necessary in order to achieve our goals. When you think about the things in your life that have given you the greatest satisfaction, they most likely involved some amount of struggle or suffering.

If you are like most people, you probably experience more happiness in your life than meaning. In general, people are happy. If we were to measure happiness on a scale of 1 to 10, the majority of us would score around 6, 7, or 8.[26] Fewer of us experience meaning in life. One study found that 75 percent of participants had high happiness scores and low meaningfulness scores, while only 25 percent had more meaning in their lives than happiness.[27]

Enhancing Well-Being

My message throughout this chapter is that well-being depends both on feeling good and doing good. Unfortunately, women often end up trading one dimension of well-being for the other. Outdated workplaces, lack of support, and traditional societal norms make it hard for us to raise a family and commit to a career at the same time. Women who are working may sacrifice some joy for the satisfaction of achieving their career goals. The difficulties of attending to both career and family demands lead to greater stress and, as a consequence, fewer positive emotions.

Women who choose to opt out of their careers in order to stay home with their children may experience more happiness because they don't face the daily hassles of combining work and family; however, they may not feel satisfied with their lives because they aren't developing their strengths or pursuing personal goals. Despite deriving a significant amount of meaning from parenting, many women yearn to make other types of contributions.

Patsy Fox had worked for some big-name companies, such as Disney, FedEx, and Hewlett-Packard, before landing a position managing European business development for DreamWorks in 1999. She and her husband were both from the United States, but they loved living in London. Patsy took a 12-week maternity leave after their first son was born, then found a nanny so that she could return to her fast-paced job. But things changed a couple of years later when their second son was born with Down syndrome. As much as they had enjoyed living in London as a couple without children, they now worried about the smog and missed having a yard where the kids could play. They also decided it would be nice to live closer to family. So Patsy and her husband quit their jobs and moved to Colorado, a place they both loved that was located between their two families.

Although Patsy was happy staying home with her children, she felt something was missing. She had always enjoyed her work and the sense of purpose it gave her. It wasn't long before a colleague from DreamWorks contacted Patsy to see if she would be interested in joining the small entertainment company Anchor Bay Entertainment, where he was currently working. Patsy jumped at the chance. The position was a far cry from her past jobs, but it allowed her to work from a home office and set her own schedule. She was able to have lunch with her children and greet the therapists who came to work with her son, while also pursuing her passion in the entertainment business and contributing financially to her family.

A few years after moving back to the United States, Patsy and her husband adopted a baby girl from China. As a mother of three, she continues to work for Anchor Bay, considering it the perfect job for her at this point in her life. Patsy is thriving! She is happy and feels that her life has meaning. She is grateful to have a job she enjoys that also lets her be there for her children. They are constant reminders for Patsy to live in the moment. Before having a family, she explains, her life

> was a ladder and you knocked out a rung and kept going up and up. You went to undergrad, you went to grad school, you got this job, you moved up, etc. . . . And all of a sudden I have a special needs child who cannot even climb a ladder. His life is going to be about loving people and living in the moment and being happy. His line is going to be curvy and twisty. I never realized there was another way to live, and I've now applied that to my life. I'm not going straight up the ladder anymore and, you know, it's okay.

Patsy not only feels good, but she is doing good. She is living her values and using her strengths to make positive contributions to her family and her organization.

What about you? Are you thriving? Or is there something missing? Here is a brief assessment to determine your current level of well-being.

Directions: Read each item carefully. Using the scale next to each item, ranging from strongly disagree (SD) to strongly agree (SA), circle the number that best describes you.

	SD				SA
1. I stay focused on what is happening in the present.	1	2	3	4	5
2. I am not preoccupied with the past or the future.	1	2	3	4	5
3. I notice the good things in life.	1	2	3	4	5
4. There is much for which I am grateful.	1	2	3	4	5
5. I have the ability to make my future better.	1	2	3	4	5
6. I see many ways of achieving my goals.	1	2	3	4	5
7. My interactions with people are positive.	1	2	3	4	5
8. I have strong relationships with others.	1	2	3	4	5
9. My actions are aligned with my values.	1	2	3	4	5
10. I have a sense of purpose in life.	1	2	3	4	5
11. I know what my strengths are.	1	2	3	4	5
12. I have the opportunity to use my strengths every day.	1	2	3	4	5
13. I make a positive impact on others.	1	2	3	4	5
14. The work I do is meaningful.	1	2	3	4	5

Scoring

Feeling Good: Add the numbers you circled for questions 1-7. On a range of 7 to 35, where did you score? This is your Feeling Good score. The higher your score, the more likely you are to be happy.

Doing Good: Add the numbers you circled for questions 8-14. This is your Doing Good score, ranging from 7 to 35. The higher your score, the more likely you are to have a sense of meaning in life.

Well-Being: Add your Feeling Good score and your Doing Good score. This is your overall Well-Being score, ranging from 14 to 70. The higher your score, the more likely you are to be thriving.

If your Well-Being score isn't as high as you'd like it to be, don't worry! Researchers in positive psychology have been working hard to identify the factors that contribute to our well-being. You can take steps right now to increase your positive emotions and to experience a greater sense of meaning in your life. The following sections of this book describe specific strategies that you can use to feel good and to do good. I will show you how to build a joyful, meaningful life by focusing on what matters most for your well-being.

Part 2

Feeling Good

· ·

"Happiness is not something ready made.
It comes from your own actions."

—Dalai Lama

FEELING GOOD MATTERS FOR your well-being because happiness has many benefits, as discussed in chapter 2. People who experience frequent positive emotions are healthier, more sociable, more productive, more creative, and more resilient.

While your happiness is influenced in part by genetics, much of it is due to your intentional activities. Happiness is a function of your thoughts and actions, which means it is under your control. You can choose to think and act in ways that will increase your happiness. Over time you can rewire your brain to be more open and receptive to positive experiences.

In Part 2, I offer three strategies for feeling good. The first strategy, presented in chapter 3, is to be mindful by focusing your attention on the present moment. In chapter 4, I discuss a second strategy for increasing positive emotions: being grateful. We experience gratitude when we notice and appreciate what is good in our lives and in the world around us. The third strategy for feeling good, covered in chapter 5, is to be hopeful about the future, to believe that things will be better and that you can make it so.

3

Be Mindful

· ·

*"The present moment is filled
with joy and happiness. If you are
attentive you will see it."*

—Thich Nhat Hanh

I WAS AT THE base of the Durango Mountain Ski Resort in
Colorado on December 31, 2009, when I got the call. It was
my husband, who told me that our son, Alex, had fallen while
snowboarding. He asked me to meet them at the Urgent Care
Center. An X-ray revealed that Alex had broken his upper arm.
Back in Phoenix, the doctor put a heavy cast on with the hopes that
it would pull the bones back into place.

A week later Alex had a follow-up doctor's appointment.
Another X-ray showed the cast wasn't realigning the bones, so
Alex was admitted to Phoenix Children's Hospital for surgery. My
husband was in New York on a business trip, so I sat alone in the
waiting room for what they told me would be a one-hour procedure
after which Alex could go home.

The book I happened to have with me was Mark Thornton's
Meditation in a New York Minute: Super Calm for the Super Busy.

I had recently been reading about the benefits of mindfulness meditation and was curious to learn more. My natural tendency in the situation I was in would have been to be beside myself with worry. I would have been thinking nonstop about all of the things that could go wrong. But I didn't. As I read the book, I tried out some of the exercises. I breathed deeply. I repeated calming words. I stayed in the moment, trying not to let my mind wander to what-ifs. I focused on connecting with the "ocean of calm" that I learned is within us all.

When a nurse came to tell me the surgery was more complicated than the doctor had anticipated, I took several more deep breaths and continued reading about strategies for staying calm. Three hours later, Alex was out of surgery. We spent the night in the hospital, where I finished the book. Alex was on the mend, and I had discovered a new way of being. My experience had given me an immediate appreciation for the impact that mindfulness could have on my life. I decided that I would make every effort from that day forward to live more mindfully.

The aim of mindfulness is to be completely focused on what you are doing, not thinking about the past or the future or other distractions. Jon Kabat-Zinn, one of the leaders of the mindfulness movement, defines mindfulness as "paying attention in a particular way: on purpose, in the present moment, and non-judgmentally."[1] Learning to pay attention moment to moment without judging increases positive emotions.

Many of our negative emotions come from ruminating about the past or worrying about the future. Focusing on the present moment can help you to keep these negative thoughts at bay. What is happening right now is most likely neutral or mildly pleasant. If you start to think about things that didn't work out well in your past, you might generate negative emotions such as regret, blame, anger, and guilt. These thoughts can ruin this otherwise pleasant moment.

Being mindful can keep you from useless worrying about the future as well. Many of the things we worry about never come true, and time spent worrying creates negative emotions. As columnist Mary Schmich so eloquently put it in an essay for the *Chicago Tribune*: "worrying is as effective as trying to solve an algebra equation by chewing bubble gum."[2]

As you go through your day, try to notice when you have checked out and are diving into your past or fretting about the future. Each time that happens gently bring your thoughts back to the present. Pay attention to what is going on here and now.

If you are ever around children, you have probably noticed that they spend much of their time focused on the present moment. Watch them as they play on the playground, build a Lego tower, practice tying their shoelaces, or savor a chocolate cupcake. If they do get upset about something, it is usually pretty easy to calm them down by drawing their attention to something else.

Our tendency to worry more as we grow older became very clear to me when our family moved across the country. We sold our house in Arizona, packed up all of our belongings, and sent them to our soon-to-be new home in Virginia. Then we left for what I thought would be a fun-filled summer visiting family and traveling with friends. Unfortunately, we weren't able to enjoy our summer as much as I had hoped because we were all so anxious about our move. Would we love our new house as much as we loved our home in Arizona? Would the kids like their new schools? Would we find new friends who we enjoyed as much as our old ones?

Of course it is normal to be worried about the future when everything is so new and uncertain. But what's interesting is that when we moved from Spain to the United States eight years before, our children showed absolutely no signs of anxiety, even though it was a much bigger move. It took three months for our belongings to cross the ocean, and we were moving to another country with a different language and culture. But at five and seven years old the kids weren't worried about the future. They spent the summer swimming, eating ice cream, and playing games without a care in the world. At that time they were still blessed with the gift children have of living in the present moment.

Sometimes it is helpful to think about the future. I'm a big planner, which requires thinking about the future and even considering things that might go wrong so that I can be prepared just in case. I feel much more comfortable knowing what's going to happen. Planning things gives me a sense of control. Yes, I know, I can't control everything and even when I have a perfect plan things don't always go the way I expect.

But I still like to make plans. And so I spend a good bit of time thinking about the future. I plan a week's worth of meals so I only have to go to the grocery store (which I hate!) once a week. I plan our vacations in advance so plane tickets are cheaper and there are more hotel options. I plan my presentations carefully so they go smoothly. Planning is important for my peace of mind. The more prepared I am, the less stressed I get.

The problem is that it is easy to cross the line and go from planning, which is productive, to worrying, which isn't. Thinking about problems you might encounter is good if it helps you prepare for handling them. I'm always careful to pack the things I know I will need in my carry-on in case my luggage gets lost. But stressing about what I will do if the flight I'm taking next week gets canceled is pretty useless. Nor is it productive to think about even worse things that could, but most likely won't, happen to me or to a loved one.

When I catch myself thinking about something in the future I ask, "Is this helpful?" This lets me know whether I've crossed the line. If I can do something about it, then I'm planning. If I can't do anything about it, then thinking about it isn't useful. I'm worrying again. It's time to bring my focus back to the present moment.

When I interview women about their careers, I always end by asking them what advice they would give to other women. Daniela Bryan, who is a professional certified coach in California, said this: "Stay in the present. Don't worry about the future too much. I have so many clients who are in the mode of getting things done. They need to get xyz accomplished and in the process they forget that their kids are right in front of them growing up. It's more important than what happens 10 years down the road. It should really be about enjoying and appreciating what is going on right now."

Being mindful can make us feel good by helping to quiet the negative voice inside our head that is reliving the past or worrying about the future. But mindfulness is not about eliminating negative emotions. In fact, one advantage of staying focused on the present moment is that you are more likely to notice the emotions that you are experiencing in that moment. Emotions, both positive and negative, provide important information that can help us respond in adaptive ways.

Although negative emotions may be unpleasant, they can motivate us to engage in constructive behaviors. Psychologists Todd Kashdan, a colleague of mine at George Mason University, and Robert Biswas-Diener discuss the benefits of negative emotions in their book *The Upside of Your Dark Side: Why Being Your Whole Self —Not Just Your "Good" Self—Drives Success and Fulfillment*.[3] They explain that self-doubt is useful when it inspires us to aim higher. Anxiety helps us to focus. Anger can fuel creativity and guilt can motivate us to do things better the next time.

Being more attuned to our feelings allows us to better manage them. Often our tendency when we experience a strong emotional stimulus is to react immediately without thinking. Being mindful enough to notice when our emotions have been triggered allows us to take a moment before we act to decide how we want to respond. Psychiatrist Viktor Frankl, who survived the Holocaust, wrote about the importance of what he referred to as the space between stimulus and response. He said, "in that space lies our freedom and our power to choose our response. In our response lies our growth and our happiness."[4]

Have you ever regretted saying or doing something in an emotional situation? Fortunately, we can learn to stop doing this. Mindfulness helps us create distance between our emotions and ourselves. Emotions are what we feel, not who we are. We can acknowledge that a situation has caused us to feel a certain way, while realizing that we have the power to not react based on our initial feelings and instead choose a more positive way of responding to the situation.

When we are mindful we are not only more aware of our own emotions, but we are also better at recognizing other people's emotions, too. When you pay close attention to what is happening at each moment, you are more likely to notice signs that reveal the emotions of people around you. Being in the moment makes you a better listener. Really listening to what people are saying and acknowledging how they feel are excellent ways to strengthen your relationships.

So what are you waiting for? Here are some tips to help you be more mindful:

Slow Down

On a cold Friday morning in January 2007, a man pulled out his violin in a Washington, D.C. Metro station and started playing Bach. He was there for about 45 minutes while people rushed past him, many on their way to work. One man slowed his pace a bit to listen before hurrying on his way. A woman dropped a dollar in the hat without stopping. Several children tried to stop to listen to the music, but each one of their parents urged them to continue walking.

Out of more than a thousand people who passed by while he was playing, only seven stopped to listen momentarily, and 27 gave money for a total of $32.17. Not a single person applauded. The man playing the violin in the Metro station that morning was Joshua Bell, one of the best musicians in the world.[5] But people were in too much of a hurry to listen. How many things might we miss because we are too busy rushing from one place to another?

One of the first things you can do to start being more mindful is to slow down. As you go through your day, try not to rush. Make an effort to eat more slowly, to walk more slowly, to drive more slowly—doing everything just a bit slower can make a big difference. Start your day more slowly. When your alarm goes off in the morning, lie in bed for a minute and notice the sensations of your breath. Set an intention to be mindful throughout your day.

Find moments in your day to STOP:[6]

S stands for Stop. Simply pause from what you are doing.

T stands for Take a breath. Notice your breath coming in and out of your nostrils. Feel your chest expand, then contract. Take another long, deep breath. Note the sense of calm that deep breathing can trigger.

O stands for Observe. Bring your awareness to your body. What sensations do you notice? Now pay attention to any emotions you may be experiencing. How do you feel at this moment?

P stands for Proceed. Continue on with whatever you were doing.

Business and constant distractions can make it challenging to remember to be mindful once you are off and running. It helps to find cues to remind you to bring your attention to the present moment. You could set an alarm to go off at certain times or schedule breaks on your calendar. Another option is to use transitions as cues. Each time you park your car take a moment to sit in stillness before getting out. As you wait for your computer to boot up, take a moment to bring your attention to your breath. Before you pick up the phone to call someone, pause to notice how you are feeling. Practice mindfulness when you walk to meetings. Put away your phone and focus on your steps or smile at the people you pass. When you sit down to a meal take a minute to notice the colors, smells, and taste of the food. Using transitions as moments of mindfulness can significantly increase the amount of time we spend in the present moment.

Don't Multitask

Increase your mindfulness by doing only one thing at a time. This allows you to give your complete attention to any activity in which you engage. You can practice present moment awareness at any time. The key is to focus all of your attention on what you are doing. How often do you check your smartphone? Is there a sound that notifies you each time you get a new text or email message? Every time you check your phone you are checking out of the present moment.

Technology is a huge distraction, making it really hard to be mindful. Writing this book helped me learn how important it was to close down my email completely so I could focus on writing without distractions. I used to be a big multitasker. I'd eat lunch while preparing a presentation, check email while talking on the phone, chop carrots while watching the news (luckily I still have all of my fingers!), and read the latest article on work-life conflict while standing in line at the grocery store.

On the rare occasion when I was only doing one thing, my mind was usually doing something else. I would plan my day while walking the dog or driving to work. I would think about what I should blog about, what phone calls I needed to make, or what to cook for dinner. Now I try to stay present in these moments. I've found that if I set aside a specific time in my day for planning, it helps me to stay in the here and now at other times. I also practice mindfulness when I'm waiting for someone or am stuck in traffic. These are occasions that used to really frustrate me, but now I take a deep breath and try to appreciate a minute of calm. I feel grateful for a moment of being rather than doing.

Staying focused on one thing is easier when you keep distractions to a minimum. When a colleague drops by your office to tell you something, take a break from what you are doing, look up from your computer, and silence your phone so you can really listen to him or her. Attentive listening helps you stay focused on the present. It also increases the positive emotions of others because they appreciate that you are listening to them. The next time you are in a meeting, keep your phone out of sight so you won't be tempted to check it.

The best way to avoid email distractions is to schedule specific times throughout the day to check your email. It might help to know that you will be much more efficient if you do just one thing at a time. Research on dual-task interference has found that your productivity can be reduced by as much as 40 percent when you switch between tasks.[7] One study showed that constant emailing and text-messaging reduced people's mental capability by an average of 10 IQ points. This effect is two to three times stronger than the effect of smoking marijuana.[8] Checking your messages less often will increase your focus and reduce your stress throughout the day.

Want to see for yourself how much multitasking slows you down? Here is an experiment for you to try. It involves performing the following two tasks: 1) write the numbers 1 through 27 and 2) write this sentence, "Do only one thing at a time." First, time yourself as you switch between tasks, write a 1, then the letter D, then a 2, then the letter o, etc. Now, time yourself performing the two tasks without switching: that is, write the numbers 1 through 27, then the full sentence.[9] It takes most people up to 50 percent less time when they perform the tasks one at a time. How about you?

Staying in the present moment when you are with your family or friends is also very important. When you are having a family dinner, turn off your phone and focus on the conversation. Go for a walk with your spouse, ask him about his day, and listen to what he says. Read a book to your children or play a game with them, without looking at your phone even once!

Many of us have to work from home. In fact, being able to work from home is exactly what many women need in order to make work work for them. If you do work from home, setting boundaries is very important. Make sure to find time to disconnect so that you can be present with your loved ones. Being mindful requires putting your work away and unplugging from your devices so that you can spend quality time with the people around you.

Connect With Nature

Spending time outside helps you to be mindful. There is so much in the natural world to engage you that it can fully occupy your attention, making it easier to keep your thoughts focused on the here and now.

I certainly notice this when I'm at the beach. I become so enthralled by the ocean that my mind doesn't wander to other things. Spending hours sitting at the water's edge listening to the waves roll in and watching the sand slowly bury my feet, I gaze at the pelicans as they fly so close to the water in perfect formation; I smile, listening to the laughter of my kids as they jump over the waves. I look for shells—sand dollars and sharks teeth are my favorite finds—and am completely focused as I walk on the beach with my head bent, searching for a treasure from the sea. When I'm at the beach, there is always another wave or bird or shell to hold my attention. I am immersed in the here and now.

You can benefit from the mindfulness that nature brings by spending time outside wherever you happen to be. Studies show that spending 20 to 30 minutes out of doors in nice weather boosts positive emotions.[10] On pleasant days, take your work outside. Sit on a bench to read the latest financial report or have a walking meeting to hear the update from your direct report. Eat lunch outside. Start that herb garden you've been thinking about. Take up golf. Explore the hiking trails near your home. Buy a hammock. Anything you can do to connect with nature will help you practice mindfulness.

Pause

When your manager stops by your office to tell you he's asked your colleague to head up the new project you had asked to lead, before telling him what you think, take a mindful pause. This will allow you to choose a thoughtful response rather than reacting blindly. Try counting to 10 or taking several deep breaths; anything that creates a space between the stimulus and your response will do. Now bring attention to the emotion you are experiencing. Reflect on where the emotion is coming from and try to reframe the situation. Often the emotion comes from your own history; perhaps something in your past has made you especially sensitive to what just happened.

Try to see the other person's point of view to better understand his perspective. Look for something positive. Ask yourself what you might learn from the situation or how it might help you grow or strengthen your relationship. Finally, consider ways you might respond to the situation that would have a positive outcome. Practice letting emotions move through you, like clouds moving across the sky. Acknowledge the emotion and then choose how you will respond.[11]

Meditate

Meditation is a more formal practice that helps you to cultivate mindfulness by training you to focus your attention. In addition to helping you to be more mindful, meditation has many other benefits—decreased stress, anxiety, and insomnia, as well as a lower likelihood of developing certain health problems such as heart disease and type 2 diabetes. It increases your self-awareness and your empathy and improves your memory.

Many people think they don't have the time or ability to meditate. But if you can breathe, you can meditate. Just a few minutes a day can make a difference. Start by setting an intention to meditate. Sit in a quiet place and focus on your breath. Notice the sensations in your body as you breathe in and out. Feel the cool air as you inhale and your chest rises and your belly expands, then, as you exhale, notice how your chest falls and warm air exits your nostrils. Scan your body from head to toe, checking for places where you might be tense and relaxing them.

If thoughts come to mind, acknowledge them and then return your attention to your breath. See how long you can stay focused. I can assure you your mind will wander. If you are breathing, you will have thoughts. The key is not to get frustrated or discouraged when you become distracted. You can't stop thinking, but you can return your attention to the present moment, refocus on your breath, and begin again and again and again.

The more you train your brain to focus attention on the present moment, the easier it gets. Some suggestions for trying to stop your mind from wandering are to count your breaths or scan your body as you focus on relaxing different body parts or repeat an affirmation such as "I'm at peace" or "All is well."

It helps to not start with an unreasonable goal. Begin by meditating for just a few minutes at a time. Each time you meditate you get a little better at it. It's a lot like going to the gym. The more you exercise your attention muscle, the stronger it will become over time. Commit to meditating every day, even if some days you only have two minutes. As it gets easier with practice, you can build up to more time. You will find that meditating makes you feel so good that you will make a point to find the time for it.

Of the many different strategies for increasing positive emotions, learning to be more mindful has probably had the biggest impact on my life. I have an achievement-driven, impatient personality—rushing around trying to do five things at once while thinking about what to do next—but I am getting much better at making intentional efforts to slow down and enjoy the present moment.

Being mindful can be very difficult in the always-on world we live in. We are so busy, overscheduled, and overcommitted that we just don't have time to slow down, to be present. And if we do, we worry that we might lose our edge or that others will think we aren't committed to success. But the truth is, doing fewer things at once makes us all more effective. Slowing down can increase our energy so we can do more. Being mindful gives us clarity to make better decisions. And focusing our attention on what we are doing at this very moment doesn't take a minute more of our time.

If you still aren't convinced of the value of being mindful, consider what Mark Muesse, one of my college professors, is fond of saying, "Life is a series of present moments. If you fail to show up for these moments, you've missed your life."

What You Can Do:

- Slow down by finding cues that will remind you to **STOP** throughout the day.

- Minimize distractions so that you can focus on doing **one thing at a time**.

- Spend time **outside**.

- **Pause** when you are emotionally triggered to choose a constructive way of responding.

- **Meditate** in order to build your attention muscle.

4

Be Grateful

· ·

"He is a man of sense who does not grieve for what he has not, but rejoices in what he has."

—Epictetus

ON OCTOBER 23, 2014, Jennifer Lockwood-Shabat told her story to a room full of people gathered at the Grand Hyatt in Washington, D.C., for the Washington Area Women's Foundation Leadership Luncheon. She grew up in a small town in Vermont where her father worked as a physician's assistant and her mother was a medical transcriptionist at the same VA hospital. When she was 10 years old, the hospital faced financial problems and both of her parents were laid off.

Her father turned to alcohol, working only sporadically, so her mother had to work two to three jobs to support their family. Lockwood-Shabat also worked multiple jobs throughout high school in order to save money for college. She ended up being the first person in her mother's family to get a college degree and went on to earn a master's degree as well.

Lockwood-Shabat is forever grateful to her mother for the sacrifices she had made so that her children would have a better life. "I do what I do because of her," she told the audience. "I've devoted my career to working on behalf of low-income women and their families because I want her to know that the investment she made in me, all of her sacrifices, were not in vain."[1]

As the president and CEO of the Women's Foundation, Lockwood-Shabat is paying forward what her mother gave her. She is leading the charge to secure resources to improve the lives of women and girls living in poverty in the Washington, D.C., region. Her work reminds her on a daily basis to be grateful for all that she has and for all that her mother did for her and her siblings.

Being grateful is noticing and appreciating all that is good. Developing an attitude of gratitude enhances your well-being by increasing the frequency of positive emotions you experience. We typically feel grateful to people because they have done something nice for us. Thinking about what they have done makes us feel good because it reminds us that someone cares about us. Gratitude has been linked to stronger marriages, improved job performance, greater compassion, optimism, forgiveness, and lower levels of stress.

Robert Emmons, a psychology professor at the University of California, Davis, is well known for his work on gratitude. In one of his studies, he and Michael McCullough, of the University of Miami, randomly assigned almost 200 students to one of three groups. The first group was asked to write down five things that they were grateful for once a week for 10 weeks. The second group was asked to write down five hassles—things that went wrong or were irritating—from the past week, while the third group listed five events that occurred in their lives over the past week, such as going shopping or getting a haircut. The people who listed what they were grateful for were more satisfied with their lives, more optimistic, and had fewer physical complaints, such as headaches, than those in the other two groups.[2]

Emmons conducted a similar study to see if gratitude might also be related to performance. As a class assignment, he had his students keep a journal throughout the semester. Some students kept a gratitude journal, while others recorded either frustrating or neutral events in their lives. In addition to being more satisfied, more optimistic, feeling more energetic, sleeping better, and having fewer physical complaints, students who kept gratitude journals were also tardy and absent less often and had higher grade-point averages than students in the other two groups.[3]

Notice the Good

"The invariable mark of wisdom is to see the miraculous in the common."

—Ralph Waldo Emerson

You can only feel grateful if you notice things for which to be thankful. Dewitt Jones was a photographer for *National Geographic* for 20 years. He says that working for *National Geographic* taught him to celebrate what's right with the world. He believes it keeps him open to possibilities and gives him—gives all of us—energy. Jones explains that when he is on a photo shoot, he always starts off by looking for what is good. When he finds it, he spends the rest of the shoot focusing on enhancing that and ignoring everything else. Jones is now a motivational speaker who uses his experience as a photographer to teach others about vision and creativity.

Unfortunately, because of our negativity bias, focusing on the positive is easier said than done. When things go well, we tend to take it for granted and not even notice. This became clear to me one day in a yoga class. Our instructor started the class by asking us to focus our thoughts on gratitude. I thought about how grateful I was that I was healthy enough to practice yoga. And that's when I realized my neck wasn't hurting anymore!

My neck had been hurting for months. It felt like a pinched nerve, and I noticed it whenever I turned my head to the right. It was especially bothersome when I was doing yoga. I had learned to live with it, but it was a constant pain in the neck. I didn't realize until that day in class that the pain was gone. I think it had been days since my neck had stopped hurting, but I hadn't noticed it. It's hard to stop thinking about what pains us, physically or otherwise. Yet when we aren't in pain, we take it for granted. We don't notice, much less appreciate, the positive nearly as much as we notice the negative.

As a mother (and a psychologist) I know it is better to reward my children for their good behavior than to punish them for their bad behavior. But let's be real. When are you most likely to notice what your kids are doing? When they are quietly doing their homework or when they are screaming and chasing each other around the house? We have to make a conscious effort to notice when something is going well and to take a moment to enjoy it.

The problem is that most of us are so busy rushing from one meeting to the next that we aren't even aware of what is going on around us. Worrying about what we are going to say to calm our client down or walking everywhere with our eyes glued to our phones keeps us from noticing the aroma drifting out of the coffee shop, or the pink sky at sunset, or the smile on a passerby's face.

Positive events are often minor, ordinary things, such as finishing something on your to-do list, a good meal, or a funny exchange with a co-worker. The key is to look for these moments and to savor them. Each time you take just a minute to stop and recognize something good, you increase the positive emotions you experience. When you notice and feel grateful for something, your brain releases dopamine, a neurotransmitter that makes you feel good. Because your brain wants more of this feel-good rush, it will start searching for things that make you feel grateful.

This means that intentionally savoring what is good, holding positive experiences in your awareness a bit longer, can train your brain to focus on the good so that gratitude becomes part of your everyday thinking pattern. As you push yourself to look for what is positive and to ignore small negative annoyances, you will replace your brain's natural tendency to focus on the negative with a preference for noticing the good. Over time, this will create new neural pathways, rewiring your brain to scan the environment for positives rather than negatives.[4]

Noticing the kindness of others can help you to feel grateful. I was heading home from a conference in San Francisco a few years ago when I almost got on the wrong train. A man nearby saw me with my suitcase in hand and warned me that the train I was boarding did not go to the airport. It was a small thing for him to do, but it sure saved me a lot of trouble. When I was finally seated in the right train, I smiled as I thought about how nice he had been to help me. A few weeks after that I was about to drive onto a busy interstate with my daughter when a woman honked at me to tell me I had a flat tire. Who knows, she might have saved our lives! Remembering these acts of kindness even today puts a smile on my face.

Intentionally looking for and noting what is good not only increases your positive emotions, but it also blocks negative emotions because we can't experience positive and negative emotions at the same time. Matthieu Ricard is a Buddhist monk who has been referred to as the "happiest person in the world" after participating in a study on happiness and scoring significantly above the average of hundreds of other participants. Ricard explains that positive and negative emotions are like hot and cold water coming out of a faucet. You can't get hot water if the cold water is also turned on. Positivity acts like the cold water in a faucet, preventing the water from getting hot; that is, preventing the flow of negative emotions.[5]

When you are at work, make an effort to focus on what is going well. Start meetings by going around the table and asking everyone to mention one positive thing that has happened recently. When you notice something good, stop for a minute and savor it so that the positive emotions really sink in. Recognize people when they do a good job. End your day by reflecting on what went well.

My sister, Katherine, really noticed the difference a positive focus can make when her team leader, Yolande, went on vacation. Katherine works in information technology. She told me how the person who took over while Yolande was away used their daily meetings to look at all of the tasks that were incomplete and to discuss the problems the team was having. It wasn't until then that my sister realized how much more motivating their meetings were under Yolande's leadership. She always started their meetings by discussing the progress the team was making and the things they were doing well.

It's important to notice what is good at home, too. Go around the dinner table and have everyone share one thing that went well that day. I also try to notice and appreciate all the little things that go well throughout my day. For example, when my son cleans the kitchen after he's made his delicious apple pie, or the rain holds off until I've had a chance to walk the dog.

When something good happens, don't just notice it. Take 10 seconds to really take it in, to extend the nice feeling, to savor the moment. Count down from 10 as you allow the good you are feeling to expand and sink in. Your daily experiences depend on how you choose to focus your attention.

Look around you right now. Find something that is good. It could be the rays of sun pouring through the window, your fuzzy slippers, the cat curled up on your lap, the sound of your children playing, the vibrant autumn leaves or fresh spring flowers. Whatever it is that you find, take a moment to be thankful for it.

Count Your Blessings

While simply noticing and appreciating what is good is a great way to increase your gratitude, there are more intentional practices for cultivating gratitude. Keeping a gratitude journal, like Emmons had his students do, is one way to make a habit of counting your blessings. You can do this by writing about an experience for which you are grateful. Include as much detail as possible, such as how the experience made you feel and why you are thankful for it. Another option is to list three good things that go well each day. This can be anything from your son making a good grade on his math test, to the gorgeous sunset, to finally finishing that report.

If you are like me and find it tiresome to have to write in a journal every day, don't force it. The important thing is to find some way to make counting your blessings a part of your daily routine. It could be before you fall asleep at night or first thing in the morning. You might choose to reflect on what you are grateful for on your way home from work. It's a great way to end the workday on a positive note and will help put you in a good mood by the time you get home.

Picking a moment every day to count your blessings ensures that you will remember to practice gratitude. I take a few minutes every morning as my children head off to school to think about what I'm thankful for. I start out thinking about how grateful I am for my family, then I go on to think of other things for which I am thankful. It's nice to start the day focusing on all the good in my life.

Another possibility is to put a screen saver on your computer that reminds you to count your blessings or to set an alarm on your calendar that goes off once a day as a reminder. Some religions practice a threshold ritual, where you think about what you are thankful for each time you enter your home. It doesn't matter what it is, as long as it reminds you to count your blessings.

Express Gratitude

"Feeling gratitude and not expressing it is like wrapping a present and not giving it."

—William Arthur Ward

Expressing gratitude to others also boosts your positivity. Yet in a gratitude survey of over 2,000 people in the United States commissioned by the John Templeton Foundation, respondents reported thinking about what they are grateful for more often than they express it. Fifty-one percent said they think about what they are thankful for each day, but only 49 percent express gratitude on a daily basis to their spouse or partner and 37 percent express thanks to their children. Just 15 percent express gratitude to their close friends on a daily basis.[6]

Despite the amount of time we spend at work, the workplace is where we are least likely to express or receive gratitude. In the same survey, only 10 percent said they express gratitude to their colleagues on a daily basis, although 88 percent reported that expressing gratitude to a colleague makes them feel happier and more fulfilled. And 74 percent never or rarely express gratitude to their manager.

It doesn't take much to say thank you or send a short email of appreciation to someone you work with. Thanking your spouse or children for small things is an easy way to make you all feel better. You might also consider sending an email of thanks to someone whom you appreciate or calling someone from your past who may not realize they did something for which you are grateful.

If you feel shy about reaching out, that's OK. It turns out that simply writing a letter of thanks to someone without ever sending it is enough to increase your positive emotions. Pick someone who has been especially kind or helpful to you, but whom you have never properly thanked, like your sister, a former teacher, or a colleague. You could even choose someone you don't know personally, but who has influenced your life, such as an author or a role model. Write a letter telling him or her how grateful you are for what he or she has done for you. You don't have to share the letter, but you should certainly consider it.

Several years ago I mentioned the benefits of expressing gratitude in a class I was teaching on positive leadership at the Thunderbird School of Global Management. When the class was over, David Kralik, one of the students, came up to me to suggest that I read his uncle's book, *365 Thank Yous*.[7]

John Kralik was at a low place in his life at the beginning of 2008. He was going through a difficult divorce, his law firm was losing money, one client was refusing to pay his bill, another was suing him, and he had no savings. On New Year's Day, John was alone and decided to go on a long walk on the Echo Mountain trail outside of Pasadena. On that walk he had an epiphany. He realized that he needed to change his outlook and start being grateful for what he had, rather than dwelling on what he didn't have. Kralik decided to write one thank-you note every day over the next year, starting with thank-you notes for his Christmas gifts. When he finished thanking people for his gifts, he began writing notes to thank people for kind things they had done.

Writing the notes reminded John of the small things he was grateful for on a daily basis. Recognizing all of the blessings in his life and reconnecting with friends through his notes helped Kralik turn his life around. In 2009, he was appointed a judge of the Los

Angeles Superior Court. He is quick to say that it was seeing the impact on the people to whom he expressed gratitude that brought him the most joy. Receiving his simple thank-you notes let them know that what they did mattered to someone.

Reframe Situations

Tim Sanders was an executive at Yahoo! before becoming a speaker and consultant. He has written several books, the latest of which is *Today We Are Rich: Harnessing the Power of Total Confidence*, in which he quotes his grandmother: "You can't be hateful when you are grateful."[8] Gratefulness pushes fear and anxiety out of your mind, replacing it with positive emotions. Sanders has a great suggestion for increasing gratitude by turning "have-tos" into "get-tos" through reframing obligations as opportunities. This practice has really helped me to remember to be grateful. When I feel myself starting to complain about something, I try to remember to stop and deliberately look for something for which I can be grateful.

The other day, when one of my children needed something for school, the first thought that popped into my mind was, "When am I going to find time to run to the store?" But I caught myself, stopped, and redirected my thoughts to how lucky I am to be a mom and to have children who are responsible enough to tell me ahead of time when they need something. And how blessed we are that we can afford to buy what we need. And isn't it great that I have a flexible job which makes it easier to fit in a trip to the store? Pausing to reframe this seemingly small situation helped me in a much larger way.

Make a habit of feeling grateful by choosing a specific time each day to count your blessings or by setting up a reminder. Throughout the workday look for opportunities to focus on gratitude. When a colleague does something to help you, pause a moment to appreciate the gesture. Or go a step further and express your gratitude. It will make you both feel better. When you start to feel frustrated by all you have to do, try reframing the situation to focus instead on all the things for which you can be grateful.

What You Can Do:

- Make an effort to **notice and savor what is good.**

- Pick a time when you will stop every day to **count your blessings.**

- **Express your gratitude** to others.

- Turn "have-tos" into "get-tos" by **reframing obligations** as opportunities to feel grateful.

5

Be Hopeful

. . . .

"Everything that is done in the world is done by hope."

—Martin Luther

IN HER COMMENCEMENT ADDRESS at George Mason University in December 2013, Anousheh Ansari told the graduates how she had dreamed of going into space as a little girl in Iran. When she was a teenager she immigrated to the United States. Ansari studied hard to learn English and went on to earn a bachelor's degree in electronics and computer engineering from George Mason and a master's degree in electrical engineering from George Washington University. She then became a successful entrepreneur in the telecommunications industry.

Yet all the while, Ansari never gave up hope that one day she would travel into space. Since she hadn't become an astronaut, Ansari realized that her best chance of fulfilling her dream would be through the commercialization of space travel. In order to encourage companies to invest in the space industry, she and her family sponsored the Ansari X Prize, which awarded $10 million to the first nongovernmental organization to launch a reusable manned spacecraft into space twice in a two-week period.

Thanks to her support of the space industry, Ansari was invited to train as a backup astronaut for a trip to the International Space Station. Although she knew that actually going into space on the mission was extremely unlikely, Ansari believed the training would move her one step closer to her dream. So she underwent six months of intense training in Star City, just outside of Moscow. Three weeks before the launch, the person for whom she was the backup developed kidney stones and was unable to make the trip. In September 2006, Anousheh Ansari fulfilled her lifelong dream by becoming the first female and first Iranian private space explorer.

From the time she was a child, Ansari had a big dream and she never lost hope that one day her dream would come true. She believed she could achieve her dream, and she found unconventional ways of pursuing it. Worrying about things that could go wrong in the future can lead to stress, which reduces joy, but future thinking about a better life that excites you can increase your joy by bringing you hope.

Hopeful people are individuals who think the future looks bright, expecting it to be better than the present. People with hope believe they have the power to achieve positive outcomes, and this inspires them to action. They set difficult goals, plan what needs to be done, and prepare for the difficulties they will inevitably face. Because of this, hopeful people are more successful. The next sections offer some strategies for becoming a more hopeful person.

Visualize the Future

Hope is a great motivator. Excitement about the future gives you the encouragement you need to work hard to achieve it. An essential element of hope is to have a clear picture of your desired future. What do you want your life to look like five years from now?

Visualizing your ideal future energizes you to work toward it. One way to create a more vivid picture is to write about the future you dream of having. The more details you include, the better.

Visualization lets you rehearse desired outcomes by imagining the future the way you want it to be. When you visualize achieving your goals you experience positive emotions, which further increases your likelihood of success.[1] So take some time to imagine your ideal future in detail, seeing it in your mind's eye as if it already exists. But don't stop there! Wishful thinking isn't enough. For hope to happen, you also need to plan how you will achieve the future you envision.

Set Specific Goals

Hope is similar to optimism with one important difference. While both share the expectation that the future will be better, hopeful thinking goes a step further to include the realization that we are responsible for moving toward our vision. Hopeful people understand that they have to work to make their dreams come true.

The effort to turn our vision into reality starts with setting well-defined goals. Goals help us move toward our dreams by directing our effort and fostering persistence. They give us a road map to follow and help focus our attention. The more specific your goals, the better. You don't want to have too many long-term goals, or you won't be able to focus. Choose one or two goals that will be critical for helping you to achieve your desired future.

We often have trouble achieving our goals because we are so overwhelmed by thinking about how to proceed that we end up doing nothing. You are more likely to take action when you have smaller, less daunting goals. Look at your long-term goal and break it into shorter-term goals. Now start listing all of the action steps you could take to move you a little closer to your short-term goals. Try to identify small things that you can do every day.

When you start taking action and see that you are making progress toward your goals, your hope will increase even more.

Visualize your ideal future, but also imagine the steps you will take in order to achieve your goal. What effort and strategies are necessary to make it happen? What can you start doing today to make your dream a reality?

Make a Plan

After identifying the action steps that will move you closer to your goal, you need to make a plan. Deciding when, where, and how you will take those steps significantly increases the probability that you will make progress toward your goal.

In one study, college students were asked to write an essay over Christmas break. Half of them were also asked to decide exactly when and where they would write the essay. The students who were asked to make a plan were more than twice as likely to complete their essays. Seventy-one percent of them wrote the essay, compared to 32 percent of those without a plan.[2]

The best plans are *if-then* plans: *if* I am in this situation, *then* I will take this action. This is an amazingly simple, but very effective strategy. If-then planning has helped people to eat less, stop smoking, remember to recycle, not drink alcohol, and use public transportation more.

If-then planning works because it helps you to take action by creating a link between a situation, which serves as a cue, and a behavior that should follow. The cue reminds you to take action. It helps your brain automate the behavior that follows so you don't depend as much on your self-control.

I've used this strategy for years to make sure I meet my health goal of going to the gym every weekday. When the kids were younger, I took them to the bus stop every morning. That was my cue. *If* I took my children to the bus stop, *then* I would go to the gym. It made going to the gym automatic, so I couldn't look for excuses not to go. Now the kids are older and they drive to school in the mornings, so I've changed it up just a bit. *If* my children leave for school in the morning, *then* I head to the gym.

You can use this strategy to remind yourself to be more mindful. *If* I'm having a conversation with someone, *then* I will put my phone away. Or to focus on the positive by noting the progress you make each day at work. *If* it is almost time to go home, *then* I will jot down what I accomplished today. Use it to ensure that you connect with your colleagues. *If* it is Friday, *then* I will invite a co-worker to lunch. How about connecting with your clients? *If* I have just returned from lunch, *then* I will call to check in with one of my clients.

What plan can you put into place to make sure you take the steps necessary for achieving your goal for a better future?

Identify Alternatives

Whatever plan you have made, it is almost certain that something will go awry. You will face obstacles and setbacks. Hope is increased when you think of alternative solutions to achieving your goal. Ansari didn't give up hope of traveling into space when she realized she wasn't going to be an astronaut. She just looked for another way.

Hopeful people are more committed to their ultimate goal than they are to a specific path for achieving it. They understand that you can arrive at the same place via multiple paths. Knowing that you can take another route if you experience a setback increases your hope for a positive outcome.

This means that you can increase hope by brainstorming creative ways of attacking your problem to find alternative routes to your goal. After you have identified a number of different strategies, choose the one you think is best, but keep Plans B and C nearby so you can pull them out if you encounter difficulties. Having options to continue moving forward when you face obstacles will keep you hopeful. Keep working toward your vision, but remain flexible and open to alternative paths for achieving it.

Note Your Successes

Another important aspect of hope is the belief that you are capable and in control. Thinking about your past successes and the effort it took to achieve them will help you see that you are able to influence positive future outcomes as well. When you experience success, take conscious note of it and accept credit for it. Recognize that goal achievement depends in large part on planning, strategy choice, effort, and persistence, all of which are under your control.

This is easier said than done for many women. Women have a tendency not to take credit for their work, especially when working with men. In one study, researchers asked female participants to complete a task that required organizing and prioritizing emails and memos. They were told that their work would be combined with a (fictional) partner's work to determine the team's performance. When women were told that their partner was a man, 89 percent of them attributed an "excellent" team rating to their male partner. They gave more credit to the man for their successful team performance than they took for themselves. When they were told their partner was another woman, they did not give her more credit than they took for themselves.[3]

The propensity of women to underestimate their value causes many to experience the imposter syndrome. Often when women are praised for their success, instead of accepting it or even relishing it for a moment, they start thinking they are unworthy of the praise. They worry that people will eventually discover that they are imposters who lack the abilities for which they are being recognized. As comedian Tina Fey put it, you think, "I'm a fraud! Oh god, they're on to me! I'm a fraud!" Meryl Streep, who has been nominated for more Academy Awards and Golden Globes than any other actor in history, has said, "You think 'why would anyone want to see me again in a movie? I don't know how to act anyway, so why am I doing this?'" Men also experience the imposter syndrome; however, research shows women tend to experience it more often and with greater intensity.[4]

When you face moments of self-doubt or worry that people are going to discover that you are an imposter, bring to mind past successes. You are where you are because of those accomplishments. Think about what you did to achieve those successes. What strategies did you use? If you were successful then, you can do it again. Don't set unrealistic goals of perfection. Accept that you don't need to know everything or be able to do everything; celebrate what you do know and what you do well.

Sometimes it helps to write about an accomplishment you are proud of and how you achieved it. Another idea is to write a "victory log," where you list all of the successes you have had in life. Think about different areas of your life, when you were a student, the relationships you've had, your career, your hobbies, and list all of the things you are proud of having done. Keep this log handy so you can look at it when you need to remind yourself of your accomplishments to boost your belief in yourself.

Find Role Models

You can increase hope by identifying a role model who has achieved similar success or someone who has been an inspiration to you. Your self-efficacy is your belief in your ability to achieve a goal or outcome. It is determined in part by your own past success experiences, but is also influenced by seeing someone else succeed. Observing someone accomplish a goal can strengthen your belief in your own abilities.

Regardless of what you are trying to do, someone else has likely done it already. And there are other people whom you admire for their accomplishments, even though they may have pursued goals different from your own. Envision these people and ask yourself how they would handle the challenge you are facing, or how they might encourage you. Think about the planning, effort, and persistence that it took for them to accomplish their goals. If they were able to do it, you can, too!

Irene O'Neill found hope through role models. She told the Brain & Behavior Research Foundation that when she first noticed the symptoms of her bipolar disorder, she reminded herself that others in her family had overcome the odds to live productive lives despite also suffering from mental illness. O'Neill's father had schizophrenia and, although he was in and out of mental institutions, he managed to keep a job throughout it all in order to provide for his family. Irene's oldest sister had also been diagnosed with bipolar disorder, but was able to work as a teacher despite her challenges.

Seeing the examples set by her father and sister gave O'Neill hope that she, too, could deal with her mental illness in a way that would allow her to live a full life. When the medications she was initially given exacerbated her symptoms, Irene refused to take them and spent time in and out of hospitals. But she didn't give up. She explored alternative treatments, finally trying lithium, which allowed her to successfully manage her disorder. O'Neill now works as a recovery specialist in the Division of Mental Health at the DuPage County Health Department outside of Chicago. She is also the president and co-founder of the Awakenings Project, which showcases art created by people with mental illness.[5] Irene found hope and inspiration seeing how her father and sister had managed their own mental illnesses. She maintained hope by recognizing that it was necessary to explore alternative paths in order to find the treatment that would ultimately work for her.

Sue Williams and Victoria Wang understand how important it is for women to have role models. An unlikely partnership arose when Williams, a director and documentary film producer, and Wang, a former banker and marketing consultant, joined forces in 2011 to create the Story Exchange. It is a nonprofit media organization dedicated to telling the stories of entrepreneurial women who are breaking through barriers to make a difference. They continually add new videos of personal startup stories to the site with a goal of collecting a thousand in all.[6]

The Story Exchange provides role models for women by showcasing the struggles and successes of hundreds of female entrepreneurs from around the world. For example, you can watch videos of Lysanne Tusar telling how she moved from Vancouver to start the first winery in Hong Kong and of Alison Chung explaining how the digital forensics company she started in Chicago helps investigate cases of fraud, theft, and corruption. Austin mom Adriana Rodriguez shares her story of fulfilling her dream of becoming a teacher by opening a Spanish-immersion preschool in her community. Traci Phillips talks about working to put herself through college and being laid off by a technology company before starting Natural Evolutions, an electronics recycling company that recycles three million pounds of e-waste each year. Hearing these women tell their stories gives us hope that we, too, can realize our dreams.

Tracy Harsvik and her husband are a "ThunderCouple." That is how alumni of the Thunderbird School of Global Management affectionately refer to fellow graduates who get married. Given that graduates of Thunderbird often work for international companies, combining the dual careers of "ThunderCouples" can be quite complicated. Tracy and her husband are no exception.

Tracy was working as a manager for SC Johnson in London when her husband was transferred to Paris. Tracy left her job to move with him. After getting settled, she created a company called Painted Art to help artists sell their work and to organize tours of artists' studios. It let her do something meaningful, while also providing the flexibility she needed with three small children.

Although she enjoyed working in the art business, Tracy wasn't making much money, so after a few years she decided to look for other opportunities. She contacted her former manager at SC Johnson and discovered there was a position open in Paris. They were looking for someone with entrepreneurial skills and were impressed when she told them about the company she had started. Tracy was hired for what she considered a dream job, managing the brands of a large multinational company across different countries.

A few years later, Tracy's husband took a job with Microsoft and they moved to Seattle. It turns out that the man who had hired Tracy in Paris was then managing SC Johnson's Costco business in the United States. Tracy admits she "did a really good job" in her position in France, and her former manager must have agreed because he created a position for her on his team.

Tracy never gave up hope that she could continue her career, despite having to leave her job multiple times. She believed in herself and created alternative pathways, starting her own company in Paris and convincing someone to establish a position for her in Seattle.

Tracy is proud of her accomplishments, which gives her confidence that she will continue to succeed. She cautions women not to be apologetic for taking time off to have kids. "It's the right thing to do. No one should be sorry. Know your worth and be confident about what you can do for the company, even if you have had time off . . . things are possible if you just keep at it and don't give up." Keep hope alive by reminding yourself that you are capable and in control and by realizing that there is always more than one way to achieve your goals.

Becoming more hopeful will make you happier. You will experience positive emotions as you anticipate a desired future that you believe you are able to personally influence. Increase hope by visualizing your ideal future. Break your long-term goal into smaller, more concrete goals and make a plan for how you will achieve them. Identify several different pathways that you could take in case your original plan doesn't work. Boost your belief in yourself by remembering past successes and looking to others who model success.

What You Can Do:

- **Visualize** your ideal future.

- Set **specific goals** that will move you in the direction of your desired future.

- Use **if-then planning** to help you take action.

- Identify several **alternative strategies** for achieving your goals.

- Keep a **victory log** where you record all of your successes.

- Consider the effort it took your **role models** to achieve success.

Think back to Lynn, introduced in the beginning of this book. What could she have done differently to experience more positive emotions, to feel good on her way to thriving? Suppose that before going to the gym Lynn decides to stop by the store on the way home from work to get the snacks, noting how fortunate they are that their daughter made the soccer team. It was a great boost for her self-esteem and will keep her active.

Lynn hums along with the music as she exercises. She waits to check her email at the office, so no additional stress on her way to work. When the traffic backs up at a light she takes advantage of the wait to STOP, pausing to breathe deeply and note how she is feeling.

Scheduling times throughout the day to check her email allows Lynn to focus her attention on preparing her presentation. Before she knows it, it's time for lunch. Lynn is pleased by the amount of progress she has made. She thinks back to a presentation she gave earlier in the year to a prospective client. They were so impressed that they closed the deal then and there. Surely her presentation Friday will be equally successful. This leaves her feeling energized and ready to face the rest of the day.

When she gets home, Lynn sits with the kids for a bit to hear about their day. Then she focuses on preparing dinner. When they sit down to the table, each person shares the best thing that happened to them that day. Their son is especially excited that he and his best friend are partners for the science project, and the family spends some time brainstorming project ideas for him. Then Jeff tells a funny story about one of his science projects that went terribly wrong. Before going to sleep, Lynn takes a small notebook from her bedside table and writes down three good things that happened that day. So much to be thankful for!

Part 3

Doing Good

. . . .

> *"The mystery of human existence lies*
> *not in just staying alive, but*
> *in finding something to live for."*
> —Fyodor Dostoyevsky

FEELING GOOD IS IMPORTANT for your well-being, but it isn't enough. People who are thriving not only experience frequent positive emotions, but they also see their lives as meaningful. They sense they are doing good because they are doing things that matter.

The feeling that you are doing good comes from being engaged in goals that are personally meaningful because they are aligned with your values or give you the opportunity to develop your strengths. You also sense that you are doing good when you pursue activities that make a positive impact in the lives of others. Your life has meaning when what you do makes a difference.

Part 3 presents three strategies for boosting your sense of doing good. In chapter 6, I discuss aligning your actions with your values and discovering your purpose. People who know what they value most and whose behavior is congruent with their values experience meaningful lives because they are living authentically. In chapter 7, I explain how developing your strengths is another way to feel you are doing good. Learning and growing in order to perform at your best gives you a sense of satisfaction. Chapter 8 addresses the third strategy for moving higher on the doing-good dimension: making a positive impact. Going beyond your own self-interest to make a difference in someone else's life is one of the most powerful ways to feel you are doing good.

6

Live Your Values

· ·

*"When your values are clear to you,
making decisions becomes easier."*

--Roy Disney

VALUES ARE DEEPLY HELD beliefs about what is right and
good, what you are willing to invest in or defend. Your
values determine which activities you will find interesting
and personally meaningful. You have the sense that you are doing
good; that is, doing the right thing, when you are authentic or true
to yourself. You are living authentically when the choices you make
and the actions you take are aligned with your values.

Making decisions is less complicated when you know your values
and choose to be authentic. The clearer your values are, the easier it
is to decide between different options. When our family moved from
Spain to Arizona, I was excited about living in the Southwest. I would
be closer than I had ever been to the West Coast and two vacation destinations that I have always wanted to visit: Napa Valley
and Hawaii. Finally, we would live close enough to visit them both!

Eight years later, as we were packing up to move back to the
East Coast, I still hadn't been to Napa or to Hawaii. It turns out

that every time we planned a vacation we chose to head back east to visit family, either my family in Alabama or my husband's family in Spain. That's because family is one of my core values and, fortunately, it is also one of my husband's core values. As attractive as it sounded to plan a trip to Hawaii, it just wasn't a priority. When we had time off, we wanted to spend it with our loved ones who lived so far away. I still hope to smell the Hawaiian flowers and sip a glass of pinot noir on a porch overlooking a Napa vineyard one of these days, but I don't regret for a minute having made choices that were aligned with what I value the most.

Clarify Your Values

In order to live your values by aligning your actions with what you care most deeply about, you must first clarify your core values. Here are a few exercises that can help you to explore your values. Try one or two of them to get you thinking about what matters most to you:

- **Life decisions**—Identify a couple of key life decisions you have made, like changing jobs or leaving a relationship. Consider what made the choice difficult. Why did you select the chosen option? Your values most likely drove your decision. Or perhaps you did what someone else wanted you to do and later regretted the decision because it didn't align with your values. Try to identify the values that influenced these important life decisions.[1]

- **Heroes**—List some of your heroes or role models; people whose stories you admire. For each of them list their characteristics that inspire you. The resulting list can give you clues as to what you believe is important: compassion, courage, and authenticity, for example.[2]

- **Life images**—Take 10 to 12 photos of things that you believe make your life meaningful. Describe how each one contributes to your life's meaning.[3]

You have many different values, but some are more important to you than others. Prioritizing them can help you focus on your core values. A common values clarification exercise is to read through a list of values and choose the ones that are most important to you. Using the list below, circle your top 10 values. This may seem like a daunting task; don't over think it. Just circle the ones that really resonate with you as you read through the list.

Now cross out five, leaving the five values that are most important to you. Rank these values from one to five in order of importance.

Achievement	Forgiveness	Power
Adventure	Freedom	Purpose
Authenticity	Friendship	Reason
Autonomy	Fun	Recognition
Balance	Giving	Respect
Beauty	Growth	Responsibility
Challenge	Health	Risk taking
Collaboration	Helpfulness	Safety
Commitment	Honesty	Security
Communication	Humility	Self-esteem
Community	Humor	Serenity
Compassion	Integrity	Simplicity
Competence	Joy	Spirituality
Contribution	Justice	Stability
Courage	Kindness	Status
Creativity	Knowledge	Tolerance
Decisiveness	Learning	Tradition
Discipline	Love	Truth
Diversity	Loyalty	Vitality
Drive	Nature/Environment	Wealth
Efficiency	Openness	Wisdom
Empathy	Order	*Insert your own value:*
Family	Patience	_____
Fairness	Peace	_____

Align Your Behavior

Holding certain values does not necessarily mean that you behave in ways that are aligned with those values. The sense that you are doing good comes when your actions are congruent with your values. You are living your values. What about you? How closely are your actions at work aligned with your core values? What about in your personal life?

List your top five values in the spaces below. Now rate how consistent your behavior has been with each of your values during the past week.

If you discover that you aren't acting in ways that promote your values, you have an opportunity to boost your well-being by more closely aligning your actions with your values.

Value	Behavior				
	Not at all consistent				Completely consistent
_____	1	2	3	4	5
_____	1	2	3	4	5
_____	1	2	3	4	5
_____	1	2	3	4	5
_____	1	2	3	4	5

Consider ways in which you could live a more authentic life by better connecting your behavior with your values. What are some concrete steps you could take to live your values? Imagine that one of your core values is health. What goals could you set to live a healthier life? Maybe you'd like to try to get to the gym three days a week. What about eating better? Think of the barriers that prevent you from living a healthier life. For a lot of us, time is a big factor. We don't have time to get to the gym or to prepare healthy meals. If health is important to you, then it is worth finding time to live a healthier life. Schedule trips to the gym on your calendar to make exercise a priority. Don't buy unhealthy food so you aren't tempted to eat poorly. Spend an hour on Sunday afternoon preparing healthy meals and snacks that you can eat throughout the week.

Often we fail to live our values because we are too busy trying to live up to someone else's expectations. Maybe personal growth is one of your core values. But since your children were born and you quit your career to stay home with them, you feel like you are stagnating. You miss being challenged and learning new things. You try not to listen to that voice inside of you pushing you to sign up for that graphic design course. As much as you would love to learn more about this field that has always fascinated you, it would be selfish to leave your family two nights a week. And you would have homework that would also take time away from your kids. You worry that your husband and children might not see you as a good mother, that you won't be living up to their expectations.

It isn't always easy to live in accordance with your values, but it is extremely important for your well-being. Talk to your loved ones about your values. If they know how much you care about something, they might be willing to make small sacrifices to allow you to increase your well-being by doing good. Discussing the importance of living your values may also encourage them to start acting more in line with their own values. Modeling authenticity in your own life could influence those around you to do the same.

Sometimes we aren't living our values because they have changed over time. New experiences and new life circumstances can affect your priorities. So it is useful to reexamine your values from time to time. It may be that advancing in your career was one of your top values, but now that you are a mother, you value family time more than climbing the corporate ladder. This could mean that a job that was more aligned with your values before is no longer satisfying.

That's what happened to Allison O'Kelly. After receiving her MBA from Harvard Business School, she was working as a high-level executive at Toys "R" Us when her first son was born. She explains in an interview on workingmother.com that it didn't take her long to realize her job didn't fit her life as a new mom, so she quit. But O'Kelly didn't stop working. She loves to work. She just knew that she needed to leave the traditional workforce.

O'Kelly started looking for companies willing to give her contract work that she could do from home. Eventually she had more work than she could handle, so she gave some of the jobs to friends who also happened to be mothers of young children. Her friends loved the part-time work, and the companies loved the work they were doing. So in 2005 O'Kelly founded Mom Corps, a company that matches professionals with companies offering flexible positions. After becoming a mother, O'Kelly found a new way of working that allowed her to spend more time in her new role that she so valued. She is also giving thousands of other parents the opportunity to do the same.[4]

Discover Your Purpose

When I was a freshman in college, I struggled with choosing my major. I thought psychology was really interesting, but I have always been very practical, so I decided to major in business administration. I assumed I would have an easier time finding a job if I graduated with a degree in business. Was that a mistake! I now know that I should have chosen to study something I liked. If you enjoy doing something, it is highly likely that you are using your strengths. You excel when you use your strengths because they are built on natural talents. You also tend to spend more time doing things you like, which helps you to improve. Becoming really good at something is a much smarter way of preparing yourself for a successful career than pursuing something just because you think it will be easier to find a job.

The second semester of my senior year, a lot of companies came to campus to interview those of us who would be graduating soon. As I had suspected, many of them, mostly banks and accounting firms, were looking for business majors. After I had several successful interviews, my parents called to see how things were going. It wasn't until that point that I realized how unhappy the prospect of working in business made me. My internship at a bank had made it even clearer that I was heading down the wrong career path.

My parents convinced me to make an appointment with the career counselor on campus. In one of our meetings she asked me directly what I wanted to do. I told her I wanted to do what she was doing. I wanted to work with people, not numbers. I wanted to help people. That revelation led me to enroll in graduate school to study, you guessed it, psychology. I focused on work psychology, which allowed me to apply some of what I had learned as a business major.

I went on to become a professor of human resource management and organizational behavior. But it took me several more years to finally discover my life purpose. For a long time, I was focused on getting tenure, which was more of a long-term goal than a purpose. I did whatever research I could to publish enough articles in good enough journals so that the university would grant me tenure. Looking back now, I realize that I was always drawn to research that focused on how to help employees be more successful and have greater well-being. But it wasn't until after I earned tenure that I started doing research that was more aligned with my values and that I felt made a positive impact.

My research in women's careers drove me to want to work with companies to change their structures and cultures so that women could more easily fulfill both their work and nonwork responsibilities. Learning about the importance of positive emotions and purpose for well-being and success gave me an even stronger desire to encourage companies to create positive workplaces where everyone could thrive.

That is what finally led me to the realization that my life purpose is to help people thrive. Whether it's working to change organizations where so many of us spend so much of our time; empowering individuals by teaching them strategies for greater joy and purpose; helping members of the George Mason University community build lives of vitality, purpose, and resilience; or doing what I can to help my family flourish, I spend most of my days trying in some way to boost people's well-being.

Your life purpose comes directly from your most central values. It is a core part of your identity that influences your goals, directs your efforts, and guides your decision making. Purpose is why you are here; it is what you want to achieve with your life, the legacy you want to leave behind. It isn't a specific goal that you can attain. It is something you will always be working toward.

Most of you are probably like me; it has taken time for you to discover your purpose. Or perhaps you are still trying to figure yours out. For other people, like Rosemary Trible, a transformative life event helped them to clarify their purpose. On a beautiful fall afternoon in October 2014, Trible stood in front of a group of students and faculty at George Mason University. Wearing a bright yellow jacket and a huge smile, she started to tell her story. In her twenties, Trible was happily married and working in a career she loved as a television talk-show host. Then her world was turned upside down when she was raped at gunpoint. Her rapist told her he knew where she lived and would kill her if she told anyone. As soon as he was gone, Trible called the police. They never found the man who attacked her, and his threatening words caused her to live in fear for years. As she puts it, he stole her joy.

Trible's experience led to her life purpose of helping others who have been wounded by abuse. She founded Fear 2 Freedom, a nonprofit organization dedicated to bringing hope and healing to people who have been harmed by sexual assault. Fear 2 Freedom partners with universities, hospitals, and communities to assemble aftercare kits for those who have been sexually assaulted or are victims of domestic violence. They also work to promote understanding in order to empower others to help those who have been abused and to find a solution to stop the abuse. Trible's purpose in life is clear: She exists to radiate joy and to restore joy to survivors of sexual violence. As she spoke about her purpose, her hand patting the gold "joy" lapel pin on her bright yellow jacket, she did in fact radiate joy.

Your life purpose may be to inspire the love of music in children, to reduce the threat of climate change, or to make a positive difference. Whatever it is, your purpose will guide you to pursue meaningful goals throughout your life. Perhaps you will teach music in an elementary school and later create a website with fun, musical activities for kids. Maybe you will start a recycling program in your neighborhood and then work to find ways that your company can reduce its carbon footprint. You may pursue your purpose by making someone's day a little better when you deliver a skinny vanilla latte with a smile or by creating a loving home environment for your children.

If you don't have a clear idea about your purpose, spend some time thinking about what you value most. Reflect on the experiences you have had that have been most meaningful to you.

Be curious and explore new things until you find something that resonates with you. Keep moving toward things that appeal to you, that give you energy.

Finding your purpose is a journey. Don't feel the need to rush things. Give yourself time. Try new experiences and also tune in to your innermost desires. Look to other people who are pursuing their purpose and see if they inspire you in some way. Engaging in meaningful goals that are aligned with your values and discovering your life purpose increase your well-being. You feel more satisfied with your life when you are doing good by doing what you feel you were meant to do.

What You Can Do:

- Pick an exercise or two that can help you to **clarify your values.**

- **Align your behavior** with your values.

- Spend time reflecting on your values and experiences in order to **discover your purpose.**

7

Develop Your Strengths

. . . .

*"Each person's greatest room for growth is in
the areas of his or her greatest strength."*
—Donald Clifton

ROBBIE SCHULDT STUDIED ADVERTISING at the Thunderbird School of Global Management. After graduating, she worked for a number of advertising agencies in New York City, where she met her husband. When he was transferred to northern Virginia just before they married, Robbie found another job in advertising in the Washington, D.C., area. It wasn't easy, but she managed to stay with the company when her husband's job moved them again, first to Atlanta and then to Detroit. She finally left that job after their daughter was born, but found another in less than a year.

Robbie's husband, who works in the automotive industry, was then transferred to Japan. It didn't take Robbie long to find a marketing position with AT&T. They lived in Japan for a few years, and she learned a lot about the culture. When they moved yet again, this time to California, Robbie combined her knowledge of Japanese culture with the communication skills she had honed in the advertising world to give presentations to families moving to Japan. Disney was building a new amusement park in Tokyo, so she had plenty of work.

While she and her family were in California, Robbie had an accident and broke both of her ankles. As part of her rehabilitation, she started working out at a health club and discovered a love of fitness. While becoming certified as a fitness instructor, she heard about an opening in marketing for the fitness chain and became the regional marketing director.

A year later, Robbie's husband was transferred back to Japan. Soon she was teaching fitness classes and making presentations about Japan via conference call to people around the world who were moving there. Robbie also continued to use her advertising skills as a marketing consultant for the Foreign Buyers' Club, a food service company.

Robbie and her family returned to the United States for a few more years before moving to Seoul, South Korea. She is currently on the board of the Seoul International Women's Association and works to coordinate tours around Seoul for newcomers and visitors to learn about the city and its culture. She also continues to teach fitness classes. Despite the challenges of moving around the globe for her husband's job, Robbie has always found opportunities to develop her strengths in meaningful ways. Her diverse experiences helped her to discover and apply new strengths, too.

Do you use your strengths often? Your sense of doing good is greater when you do things that let you be authentic by using your unique combination of talents. We develop our strengths by investing in our natural talents, practicing them and acquiring skills and knowledge to support them. We feel energized when we use our strengths. Because they come naturally, applying strengths is easy and enjoyable. People who use their strengths every day are happier and perform at their very best.

Using your strengths increases positive emotions such as joy, satisfaction, fulfillment, and pride, so developing your strengths can move you higher on the feeling-good dimension of well-being. Simply discovering what your unique strengths are gives you emotional satisfaction. People who know what their strengths are and have the opportunity to use them often are more likely to be happy.

But the main reason a strengths focus is important for our well-being is that developing our strengths increases our sense of doing good. We feel authentic when we use our natural talents, and our greatest opportunities for success come from applying our strengths. Developing our strengths lets us be more of who we truly are.

Building on strengths is more productive than trying to improve upon weaknesses because investing in strengths typically leads to much greater improvements than making comparable efforts to enhance weaknesses. For example, when a group of students participated in speed-reading classes, the students who were the fastest readers before taking the class improved their reading ability significantly more than did the slower readers.[1]

Identify Your Strengths

In order to do good by developing our strengths, we first need to know what they are. Because they come so naturally, we often take them for granted, assuming they come as easily to everyone else as they do to us. Researchers estimate that as many as two-thirds of us have no idea what our strengths are.[2] Three ways to learn about your strengths are self-discovery, assessments, and feedback from others.

Self-Discovery

Four clues will help uncover your strengths:

1. **Enjoyment:** Experiences that bring about positive emotions often point to a strength. We typically enjoy doing what we are good at. It can be exciting to use one of

your strengths to meet a challenge. Rachel Ray seems to be having a great time when she is cooking, doesn't she? When you engage in an activity that satisfies you, it is likely that you are using a strength. What do you like to do in your free time? My brother-in-law is a cartoonist who spends his days drawing pictures for his books. He clearly loves what he does because when we are on vacation together he spends much of his time drawing.

If you experience timelessness when performing an activity, it is an even stronger sign that you are using a strength. Have you ever had so much fun doing something that time seemed to just fly by? Being so engaged in an activity that you don't notice the passing of time is another sign that you are applying a natural strength.

What you enjoyed doing as a child is another sign of a strength. Did you have a strong desire to learn something or to participate in a particular activity? We sometimes have an internal push that moves us to engage in certain activities. We feel drawn to do them because they give us joy. These yearnings from childhood are especially strong signs of a strength.

2. **Ease:** Another clue to your strengths is the ease with which you can do something. When you are good at something, you usually pick it up pretty fast. Can you think of a time you tried to learn something new and it just seemed to come naturally? You figured it out quickly and with little effort? Rapid learning is a good sign that you were using one of your strengths.

Your spontaneous reactions come so easily to you that you don't even think about them. They also point to strengths. How do you react in an emergency situation?

Do you take charge immediately, assigning people tasks that need to be done? Do you insist on getting as much information as possible before deciding how to proceed? Do you use your humor to help others cope? Your initial gut reaction in situations like this very likely reveals a strength.

3. **Excellence:** More evidence pointing to your strengths are things you do extremely well. When you really excel at something you can be pretty sure that you are using a strength. Repeated patterns of successful performance are most likely to occur when using a strength. Recall three or four peak moments from your past when you performed at your very best. Now try to identify common themes from the different moments. Were you using the same strengths in any of the situations?

4. **Energy:** Probably the biggest difference between using a strength and using a weakness is that using a strength energizes you while using a weakness drains your energy. You feel invigorated when you are applying a strength. As a result, you tend to put tasks that draw on a strength at the top of your to-do list and you almost always manage to finish them. And when you are done you feel great! You might even feel like you have more energy than when you started.

One of the best ways to discover what you enjoy, what comes easily to you, what you excel at, and what energizes you is through experimentation. Experimenting also helps you figure out what you don't like to do. In her book *Working Identity: Unconventional Strategies for Reinventing Your Career*, career expert Herminia Ibarra argues that the best way to learn about yourself is by doing. So take a photography class or a writing class. Volunteer to work at the local animal shelter or start taking master gardener classes. Offer to design websites for friends and family members. Look for a freelance assignment in a new field. Playing with different experiences is a wonderful way to discover your strengths.

Assessments

Another way to uncover your strengths is to take a strengths assessment. There are three assessments that you can complete online to identify your strengths:

1. The Values in Action or VIA Inventory of Strengths is a free questionnaire that measures 24 character strengths. They are grouped into six categories: Wisdom and knowledge, Courage, Humanity, Justice, Temperance, and Transcendence.[3] The survey can be found at www. viasurvey.org.

2. The Gallup organization has an assessment called StrengthsFinder. This survey measures 34 signature themes, which represent natural ways of thinking and behaving. They can be developed into strengths through practice and acquiring relevant skills and knowledge. For more information, go to www.gallupstrengthscenter.com.

3. A third inventory, R2 Strengths Profiler, was developed by the Centre for Applied Positive Psychology. The items in this survey assess 60 strengths based on energy, performance, and use. Results identify realized strengths, unrealized strengths, learned behaviors, and weaknesses. The assessment can be taken at www.cappeu.com/ R2StrengthsProfiler.

Realized strengths are things that you do well, that energize you, and that you do frequently. Unrealized strengths are things you do well and that energize you, but you aren't currently using them often. Learned behaviors are also things you do well, so you sometimes confuse them with strengths. Think of the things you have learned to do at work through training and experience. You may have learned to do a number of things well; however, if you aren't using a natural strength, doing them can drain your energy, which can lead to burnout. Weaknesses are things that you don't do well and that also drain your energy.

While all three assessments provide a measure of positive qualities that you can work to develop in order to be your best, there are a number of differences. The VIA Survey measures strengths of character, your core personality characteristics, with the goal of helping you live a more virtuous life. The idea is that if more people exercised these strengths, the world would be a better place. StrengthsFinder has more of a performance focus. It is often used to help people think about which careers they might excel in or how to improve their performance at work. There is a leadership version of the assessment that provides strategies for leading with your strengths. R2 Strengths Profiler is the only assessment that includes learned behaviors and weaknesses. It also identifies unrealized strengths, which can serve as a guide for where to focus your development efforts.

Feedback From Others

A final option for discovering your strengths is through feedback from others. One way to do this is to review the performance evaluations you have received over the years. Do you see any common themes? It is often the case that different managers will notice you using the same strengths, even across the diverse roles you have had.

Another way to get information about your strengths is through the Reflected Best Self (RBS) exercise. When she was a professor at the Harvard Business School, Laura Morgan Roberts and her colleagues developed this exercise to help people uncover their strengths by seeking feedback from others.[4] The exercise involves three steps:

The first step consists of collecting feedback from people who know you. You should include a variety of people inside and outside of work, such as friends, family members, and current and past colleagues. Ask them to recall specific incidents and stories about when they have seen you at your best. Ask them to give positive feedback about your strengths and how you have applied them. People are typically happy to give you positive feedback.

Once you have gathered all of the stories, the second step is to read through the feedback and search for common themes. It helps to organize the information by making a table listing the themes with the examples given and your own interpretation. You might be surprised to find that despite having solicited feedback from a wide range of individuals, the comments are typically quite consistent because they all point to your unique strengths.

The third step of the RBS exercise is to compose a self-portrait. In this step you write a description of yourself based on the information you have gathered and summarized. Writing a short narrative will help you to make sense of different events in your past, connect different themes, and come to a deeper understanding of who you are at your best.

The RBS exercise not only helps you identify your strengths, but the feedback you receive from your friends, family, and colleagues will also boost your positive emotions. I often assigned this exercise to my students and asked them to write about the experience. Many of them expressed how moved they were when they read the stories people shared about seeing them at their best. So save the feedback you get and reread it in the future when you face difficult moments. Better yet, add it to your victory log.

Apply Your Strengths

Now that you have identified your strengths, you need to create opportunities to use your strengths more often in order to develop them further. If your strength is relationship building, look for opportunities to connect with others. Take the time to get to know them in order to deepen your relationship. Look for someone you could mentor at work. If curiosity is one of your strengths, buy a book on a subject you know nothing about or try a new restaurant the next time you go out to dinner. Ask questions at meetings to help people explore alternative ways of achieving the team's goals. If your strength is focus, take one of your goals and make a detailed plan of how you will achieve it. Prioritize the steps you need to take. Revisit your plan often to assess your progress and make needed adjustments.

If you work outside the home, it is important to find ways to use your strengths as often as possible throughout the workday. One strategy for increasing the likelihood that you will be able to apply your strengths at work each day is role shaping. Complementary partnerships and strategic volunteering can help you develop your strengths either at work or outside of work.

Role Shaping

Look for ways to reshape your job in order to create a better fit between your work and your strengths. Jobs are rarely designed based on a person's unique combination of strengths, so talk to your manager about modifying your roles. Because no two people are exactly alike, people in the same job will naturally assume somewhat different roles and adopt different approaches for accomplishing their objectives. Role shaping can help to enhance the fit between your strengths and the tasks you perform.

For example, one of Rebecca's tasks as program office administrator was to prepare a monthly progress report that included financial information for each of the projects in the program. Finance was one of her strengths, so she developed a simplified procedure that made it easier for each of the project managers to report their monthly financials. When Rebecca moved to another position, Stephen took over. His strength was in graphic design, which he used to enhance the progress reports with a number of charts and graphs that made key information stand out more effectively.[5]

Viewing your job as a group of distinct tasks will make it easier to see how your role might be modified to fit your unique strengths. Often small changes can be made without altering the fixed constraints of the job. Every job has core responsibilities that are nonnegotiable, but there are typically many other tasks that can be modified or even assigned to someone else. It may just take identifying a different way of obtaining the same outcome.

There will certainly be some tasks that you will have to do that don't fall within your strengths. It is unrealistic to think that everything you do at work will allow you to use your strengths. The goal is to find as many opportunities as possible, not to eliminate every task you don't enjoy. Like the ratio of positive-to-negative emotions, the aim is to perform more tasks that allow you to apply your strengths than tasks that don't.

A few months before I went off to college, I received a letter telling me whom my roommate would be. I was so excited! We had the same middle name. Surely that was a good sign. A week or so later I received a letter from Debbie. We spent the rest of the summer sending letters and pictures back and forth, getting to know each other and deciding who would bring what for our dorm room.

Debbie and I got along great and quickly became best friends. She majored in English and eventually went to law school, where she was one of the top performers in her class, due in part to her exceptional writing skills. Last summer I talked to Debbie about her job. She was working for a law firm as an advocate for children who need extra support from the public school system. One of her main responsibilities was to attend meetings between parents and school officials. These meetings were often filled with conflict and hostility. They made her uncomfortable, and she worried that she wouldn't be successful because she wasn't using her strengths. After all, she is a writer, not a fighter!

Not long after we talked, Debbie decided to take action. She explained to her manager that she was unhappy with her job. She pointed out that her strength was writing. They discussed ways in which Debbie could modify her job so that she could spend more time doing what she does best. They agreed that she would focus exclusively on research and writing. Debbie explained to me that she "was willing to work fewer hours, because my boss didn't know how much writing they would need, but it turns out that I have done such a good job that he now lets me write briefs that he would have written."

Debbie is much happier now and feels that using her strengths allows her to make more of a meaningful impact. Her manager is also very pleased with the work she is doing and is willing to trust her with tough assignments because he knows she'll do a good job.

Sometimes you can modify your role so that it is more fulfilling by adding tasks that allow you to use your strengths. One of my yoga instructors, who happened to be a great guitar player, would bring his guitar to class. When everyone was relaxing at the end of class, he would play a song he had written. We enjoyed the live music, and his teaching was more meaningful to him because he was incorporating another one of his strengths into his work.

If you are not using your strengths at work and there is no way to modify your role sufficiently, you may want to think about looking for another position that fits you better; where your strengths will help you to succeed. There are many stories of individuals who were floundering in positions that did not let them play to their strengths, but who later flourished when they were moved into roles that relied on their strengths.

Complementary Partnerships

Many highly accomplished people owe their success to a complementary partnership. That is, they found a partner who had a different set of strengths and together they were unstoppable. Some that come to mind are Rodgers and Hammerstein, Hewlett and Packard, Lucy and Desi, Steve Jobs and Steve Wozniak, Bill and Melinda Gates, Lennon and McCartney, Oprah Winfrey and Gayle King, and Fred Astaire and Ginger Rogers, who did everything Fred did backwards and in high heels.

In his book *Working Together: Why Great Partnerships Succeed*, Michael Eisner, CEO of the Walt Disney Company from 1984 until 2005, discusses his complementary partnership with Disney president Frank Wells. They are a perfect example of complementary strengths. Eisner had the creative brilliance and Wells had the business sense. Wells once told *Fortune*, "For Michael, I make life easier. For me, he makes life more fun."

The best teams are also complementary. Ideally, team members contribute a range of different strengths. Task assignments should take into consideration the tasks that different team members enjoy, the ones they feel they can excel at, where they believe they can make the greatest contribution to the organization's goals, and the tasks they would rather avoid.

Strategic Volunteering

Look for strategic volunteer opportunities that will let you use your strengths. If finance is your thing, you might want to consider helping out your local conservation group as the treasurer. If you love interacting with children, you could teach classes at your place of worship or your community center. My father is a nature buff, with a particular love of bird watching. He has an incredible talent for spotting birds high up in the trees and recognizing their calls. Every year he takes part in the Audubon Society's Christmas Bird Count.

After she graduated from Stanford Law School, no law firm would hire Sandra Day O'Connor because she was a woman. She eventually opened her own law practice with a partner in Phoenix, Arizona, in 1958. After her second son was born, she decided to leave her practice to stay home with her children. During that time she continued to use her strengths by volunteering to work as a juvenile court referee and to write and grade bar exams for the state. The unpaid positions let her do good while she was out of work and were extremely valuable for helping the future Supreme Court justice keep her legal skills up-to-date. She also built relationships volunteering for the Republican Party, which helped her land a job in the Arizona attorney general's office in 1965. The rest, as they say, is history.[6]

What You Can Do:

- Use self-discovery, assessments, or feedback from others to **identify your strengths**.

- Look for ways to **reshape your job** in order to use your strengths more.

- Work with partners or team members who have **complementary strengths**.

- Find **strategic volunteer** opportunities that let you use your strengths.

8

Make a Positive Impact

· ·

*"A life is not important except in the
impact it has on other lives."*

— Jackie Robinson

L AURA LIBMAN, A SINGLE mom raising two children, worked
as a knowledge engineer to document the procedures developed by aerospace and industrial automation experts. Her
sense of purpose at the time came from taking care of her family,
but as her kids grew older she decided to pursue her desire to help
alleviate poverty. Laura was almost 40 when she began a master's
degree program in international development at the Thunderbird School of Global Management. She had several corporate job
offers when she graduated in 2005, but Laura knew she wanted to
do something else; she wanted to make a difference in the lives of
poor people.

Having spent summers during her youth visiting cousins on
a family ranch near Guadalajara, Mexico, Laura decided to start
searching there for a need that she could work to satisfy. She spent
two months living among the residents of a handful of small moun-
tainside towns in order to identify their greatest needs for survival.

She learned that one of their biggest problems was a lack of access to healthcare.

> *I developed a study to do while I was there, and at the end I discovered that 83 percent of the people who went from normal poverty to extreme poverty reported that the reason was a health-related incident, like a mother dying in childbirth or a farmer getting injured and not having medical supplies, so the injury turned gangrenous and he ended up with an amputation. Asking them what they needed is what gave me the idea to start with healthcare.*

Returning home to Arizona, Laura founded a nonprofit called the Tia Foundation. One day, she came by my office at Arizona State University to tell me about her project. She couldn't hide her excitement as she explained how the main focus of the foundation would be to train and equip community healthcare workers in remote Mexican villages that were hours from the nearest doctors or medical facilities. She made it clear that she wanted the foundation to provide sustainable development strategies rather than relief.

Today, the 259 health workers who have been trained by the Tia Foundation serve over 100,000 villagers, providing vaccinations, managing chronic diseases such as diabetes, delivering babies, and offering preventative education. The local governments resupply the medical kits that each health worker is given and take over continuing education, ensuring that the programs in each village remain self-sustaining.

Engaging our strengths in activities that are meaningful to us increases our sense of doing good. But we experience even greater meaning in life when we make a positive impact by serving a purpose that is larger than ourselves. Pursuing a passion is great, but passions are often self-focused—what *we* enjoy doing. According to Aristotle, our true calling is found where our "distinctive talents intersect with the needs of the world." Turning our passion into a purpose to serve others pushes us even higher up the doing-good dimension of well-being.

Detect a Need

How can you, like Laura, leverage your strengths to act out your values in service to others? By now you should have a good idea of your core values and your strengths. The next step in figuring out what kind of an impact you'd like to make is to start investigating what needs to be fixed.[1] There are many different places where you can make a positive impact. What might your loved ones, co-workers, clients, or members of the broader community need?

Laura knew she wanted to make a difference in the lives of people living in poverty. Spending time with the people she desired to help allowed her to identify a need that she could serve using her talents and education. Here are some questions you can ask to identify needs closer to home:

- **Work needs**—Think about different things at work that bother you; things you think need to be fixed. Start small, with your own work, then branch out to consider your team, your department, your organization. Write a few things for each of these domains that you would like to change. To which ones are you most drawn?[2]

- **Family or community needs**—Is there someone in your family who has a particular need that you could help with? What are two or three things you would like to change about your community? What stories have moved you recently?[3]

Write down a list of the needs you have identified. Now refer back to your values. Circle the needs that are most aligned with your core values, the ones you care most about. Next, looking at the needs that you have circled, put a star beside the ones that you feel you could address using your strengths.[4]

Voilà! You have just identified one or more ways of making a meaningful contribution. If you have several to choose from, think about which one excites you the most. Which one do you think you will have a better chance of achieving? Which one will make the biggest impact?

Michelle King Robson identified such a cause when she herself needed help. When she was 42 her doctor told her she needed to have a complete hysterectomy. She followed his advice and had the surgery. Afterward, Robson started having health problems. She saw multiple doctors who prescribed many different medications and nothing worked. Unable to find the answers she needed, she ended up suffering in silence, at one point becoming so depressed that she considered suicide. Finally, Robson found a doctor who specialized in women's health and with her help she started feeling better.

Robson's experience led her to the realization that many women face similar situations. They have health problems that they either don't feel comfortable talking about or for which they are struggling to find answers. She saw a real need. Women needed a resource where they could access information that would help them advocate for their own health. So Robson founded EmpowHER, a social media health community for women. EmpowHER helps women live healthier lives by connecting them with doctors and other women who have had similar health experiences, giving them access to reliable information and inspiring stories. It has one of the largest women's health libraries on the web and provides answers to health questions within 24 hours.[5]

Robson's personal experience raised her awareness of a need shared by others like her. Have you been frustrated by a situation that likely affects others as well? Have you heard your friends or colleagues complain about something they believe needs to be fixed? Laura Libman and Michelle Robson both started companies to address the needs they saw, but there are many other ways you can make a positive difference in this world.

I first met Patsy Mangas when she came to George Mason University to tell us about her idea of organizing a summit for girls. Patsy is a mother of four who became aware of the pressure that girls face when her eldest daughter was bullied in the eighth grade. She started noticing how girls, so carefree and full of life when they are younger, change when they enter middle school; their self-confidence starts to erode as they begin to compare themselves with others. Magazines and social media send messages that they aren't skinny enough, smart enough, or pretty enough. Bullying can result from these feelings of insecurity.

This led Patsy to invite the author of a book on female bullying to speak at her daughter's high school. She also organized a speaker series for parents. But she had bigger dreams.

> *I always had in the back of my mind that I wanted to do a summit to inspire girls, to give them a place to go and feel like they are enough, that they are good enough just the way they are, and I had seen the California Women's Conference that Maria Shriver did, and I thought, why can't we do that for girls?*

With the help of faculty, Patsy recruited university students to work with her to organize the summit she envisioned. They reached out to over two dozen girls from local high schools and middle schools who agreed to serve as ambassadors, participating in focus groups to identify the issues that were most affecting them and using social media to get the word out about the event. On November 15, 2014, after a year of hard work, Patsy realized her vision. More than 200 girls, from seventh to twelfth grades, attended the Virginia Girls' Summit on George Mason's Fairfax Campus. Many of their mothers joined them as well.

The goal of the conference was to inspire, empower, educate, and connect. The girls spent the day attending sessions to discuss how to minimize negative-self talk and discover their true identities and how to use mindfulness to quiet the noise of social media and focus on what is important to them. They had the opportunity to share their own experiences, anxieties, and hopes for the future with other girls. Patsy detected a need and took steps to address that need. She made a positive difference by organizing an event to encourage girls to listen to their own voices, to be themselves, and to follow their dreams.

Do Meaningful Work

"We make a living by what we get. We make a life by what we give."
—Winston Churchill

Work gives people the opportunity to do good by making a positive impact. It lets them coordinate their actions with others to improve people's lives by providing them with a valuable product or service. Unfortunately, many workers fail to derive a sense of meaning from their jobs. In a survey of over 12,000 mostly white-collar employees worldwide, 50 percent reported that their work did not give them a sense of meaning or significance.[6]

Amy Wrzesniewski is a professor of organizational behavior in the School of Management at Yale University. She has been studying how people find meaning in their work for over 20 years.

According to her research, people experience their work as a job, a career, or a calling. Those who view their work as a job do it mainly to earn a living. People who see their work as a career are interested in money, responsibility, and advancement. People who view their job as a calling believe what they do is of value to others. They do the work for its own sake, not for financial or other benefits. They are passionate about what they do because they believe they are making a positive difference in the world.[7]

Interestingly, whether or not people experience their work as a calling does not depend on the actual work they do. Meaning is about how we understand the work we do, not the work itself. Most any job has social value. We consider our work a calling when we recognize the value of the work we do. People can turn their work into a calling and find purpose in what they do by changing the way they view their work. A classic example of this is the person who says "I'm a bricklayer," while the person working beside him says "I'm building a cathedral to God." A dishwasher in a restaurant and a janitor in a hospital can both feel a sense of responsibility for saving lives. The cleaning they provide is critical for ensuring people's health.

Recognize Your Impact

You see your work as a calling when you recognize the impact that your work has on others. Rediscovering the ways in which your work improves people's lives can reignite your sense of meaning by reminding you that what you do matters. It is important to understand how the work you do contributes to your company's mission. It's easy to get so bogged down in your daily tasks that you forget why you are doing them. In the worst-case scenario, you have never known how your tasks make a difference. The more clearly you see how your actions benefit and are appreciated by others, the more meaning you will experience.

Unfortunately, the complexity of work today can make it harder for us to connect what we do on a daily basis to valued outcomes. We can't always see a direct link between our work and how it serves others. We may not understand how our work actually affects customers. This disconnect can reduce the perceived meaningfulness of our work.

One of the best strategies for increasing the likelihood that you view your work as a calling is to see firsthand the impact you have on others. Adam Grant, a professor of management at the Wharton School of the University of Pennsylvania, was asked to figure out how to motivate workers in a university call center whose job was to call alumni and ask them to donate money. Grant invited a student who had received a scholarship funded by the callers' efforts to talk to them. After meeting the scholarship recipient, their weekly phone minutes increased 142 percent and weekly revenue rose by over 400 percent.[8] Seeing how their actions benefited and were appreciated by someone had a significant impact on their motivation. The callers realized they were making a meaningful difference in people's lives.

Researchers in Helsinki have also shown that contact with clients can increase the meaningfulness people experience in their work. Timo Vuori and his colleagues discovered that pharmaceutical sales representatives were more likely to report experiencing meaning at work when they spoke to the physicians they served and were told the information they provided was useful. When they saw their work as helping physicians heal patients, the sales representatives felt the work they were doing was valuable.[9]

If you happen to be in a job where you are far removed from the end user of your company's product or service, try to connect with someone who benefits from your work. Experiencing the direct consequences that your work has for others will help to make your job more meaningful. When you think about your work, rather than thinking of the tasks that you perform, focus instead on the impact you are making.

Adam Leipzig is a former Disney executive who supervised films such as *Dead Poets Society*, *Good Morning, Vietnam*, and *Honey, I Shrunk the Kids*. He went on to produce many other movies and later became the president of National Geographic Films. He is currently CEO of Entertainment Media Partners.

Leipzig is a graduate of Yale University and at his 25th college reunion he was saddened to hear that so many of his friends were unhappy with their lives. It dawned on him that the people who were happy were those who felt they had a life purpose, that they were making a positive impact. This realization inspired him to give a TED Talk in which he explains that people who know their life purpose are able to answer the following five questions:[10]

1. Who are you?

2. What do you do?

3. Who do you do it for?

4. What do those people want or need?

5. How do they change as a result of what you give them?

According to Leipzig, when someone asks you what you do, your response should be what you answered to question number five. It's about how you serve others; the significance of what you do. Take a moment to answer these five questions. Remind yourself why you do what you do and try to stay focused on the impact you are making.

Day-to-day stresses can keep you focused on seemingly insignificant tasks. It can make you forget the positive impact your work has on others. Every once in a while, take a step back and look at your work in a different light. If you are a cook, think about the essential role you play in people's health or the experience you provide to customers. If you are a manager, remind yourself that you are contributing to the well-being of your team members by giving them the opportunity to use their strengths and make an impact. My sister works for Volvo Trucks; she believes that her company makes a difference in people's lives by bringing them needed food and supplies and is also proud of Volvo's commitment to safety and to the environment.

Make a Change

Laura Davis worked for Morgan Stanley in New York City for several years before co-founding a consulting business with a partner. After 10 years, she decided it was time for a change.

> *I wanted to do something else. It made less and less sense. I felt that being in the situation of having two kids and a long commute and very demanding work where I had to travel a lot was becoming less and less worth it. The higher up I got, the more important I got, the less meaning it gave me. I wanted to do something that gave me more meaning, a cause, something I could put my passion in.*

Laura left the company and spent some time thinking about what she wanted to do. She attended workshops on all sorts of subjects and took up painting. But she says, "all along I was consumed with the issue of women and work." Laura wanted to start a support group for career mothers and discovered that one already existed. Mothers & More is a network that connects mothers with other women who are facing similar challenges. Laura contacted them and set up a local chapter.

Next, she persuaded her former partner to hire her to coach women in the firm. When the two of them started the company, Laura had been the only professional woman there. It was hard to work in a male-dominated industry without any role models. She felt that she had something to offer young women.

Laura is much more satisfied with her life now. She sees the impact she is making in women's lives. Some of the women she coaches have been promoted. And she loves seeing how Mothers & More empowers women by providing them with a community, resources, and a sense of self-worth.

Margaret Barnett was moved by the number of people who attended her father's funeral. She realized how connected he had been to his community and how many lives he had touched. Margaret loved her job as an interior designer, but she didn't feel like she was making a meaningful difference in people's lives. She wanted her life to matter like her father's had.

She started looking for ways that she could use her talent as a decorator to make a difference. How could she serve the needs of people living in her community? She thought about the warehouse where she stores items that her interior design clients have discarded over the years. And that's when the idea hit her. Margaret could help people who didn't have enough resources to furnish their homes.

In 2010, Margaret formed the nonprofit What a Life Foundation to design living spaces for disabled veterans. She and her team meet with veterans and their families to learn about their needs and dream items. Then they renovate and decorate their homes, adding ramps or railings and providing any other needed goods such as beds, tables, dishes, towels, and televisions.[11] Margaret now has a strong sense of doing good because she is making a positive impact on people's lives. She found a way to live her values by using her strengths to serve others in need.

Perhaps you are having a hard time identifying the impact you are making in your current job. If so, you may want to consider making changes to increase the meaningfulness of your work. You could change careers like Laura, start something on the side like Margaret, or perhaps all you need to do is to make changes to your current job by adding or revising tasks so that you make more of a positive impact.[12] What tasks could you add that you find fulfilling? Maybe you could volunteer for a training role, which would give you the chance to make a difference by teaching others. If you are concerned about sustainability, you could lead an effort to identify ways that your company could save energy or reduce waste.

Another option is to make a difference at work through the impact you have on the people you work with. What could you do to have a positive impact on your co-workers? Perhaps you could find someone to mentor. Or you could treat a colleague who is having a bad day to lunch. A friend of mine loves to travel, and she has decorated the window of her office with flags from countries all over the world. The flags provide a colorful splash that livens up the office for everyone who walks by. She also brings baked goods to work and organizes birthday parties, baby showers, retirement parties, you name it, for all of her colleagues. She does good in many ways through her work, but one of them is by making people around her happy.

If you'd like to make more of a positive impact at work, take steps to change your tasks or your social interactions. What could you start doing that would matter to others? Even small changes can make a big difference in the way you see your work.

Of course, your work has an impact on your and your family's financial well-being, too. Mothers are now the sole or primary provider in 40 percent of American households with children under the age of 18.[13] Yet paid work isn't the only way to make a positive difference. Women also make a significant impact on the lives of others by caring for their families and volunteering in the community.

Elizabeth Coyne, or Bibi as her friends call her, lives near a beautiful old park in Winston-Salem, North Carolina. Hanes Park was given to the city on its incorporation in 1919 by P.H. Hanes, the founder of Hanes Knitting Company. The park, with its lovely bridges and stonewalls, was designed by a noted landscape architect and lauded as one of the finest parks in the South. When Bibi learned there was talk of building a high school football stadium on the park site, which had fallen into disrepair, she sprang into action.

Feeling strongly that the park enhanced the quality of life in her community, Bibi organized a group of concerned citizens, Friends of Hanes Park, who are working together to preserve and protect the historic green space.[14] They have dedicated endless hours to cleaning the park and raising awareness and funds for additional improvements. Volunteers are now busy preparing for the park's centennial celebration. They hope their work will save the park for future generations.

The way we do good evolves with our life circumstances. Right now, one of the main ways in which I make a difference is by being the best mother that I can to our teenagers. I feel that I have a direct impact on whether or not they thrive. I prepare their meals; schedule doctors' appointments; encourage them to get enough sleep, talk to them about college options; and drive our daughter to tennis practice, piano lessons, and to meet her friends. They may not admit it, but they still need me.

In a few years, my children will no longer need me on a daily basis. I'll miss them terribly, but will have more time to dedicate to my work, which I find deeply meaningful. I'll find new ways to do good, ways in which I can use my strengths to pursue valued activities that help others to thrive. It's exciting to think about the possibilities!

What about you? What makes you come alive? What is your why? How are you doing good in this world? Remember that you don't have to do something grand to make a difference. There are many ways you can do good by serving others. Even small positive interactions or kind deeds can make someone's day.

What You Can Do:

- **Look for needs** at work or in your family or community that you could help to satisfy.

- **Recognize the impact** of your work.

- **Change your tasks or your interactions** with others in order to find more meaning at work.

• •

Returning again to Lynn, what could she have done differently to experience a greater sense of doing good? For starters, getting to the gym most mornings makes her feel as though she is on the right track. She is living her values because health is important to her. Family is also one of her core values. At times, Lynn feels overwhelmed by all she needs to do, but knowing that she is making a positive impact on the lives of her children and husband gives her life meaning.

Lynn has found a greater sense of meaning at work since she talked to her manager about her job. After giving a few presentations to clients last year, she realized how much she enjoyed it, so she asked if she could give more presentations. He agreed that communication is one of her strengths and let her modify her role so that one of her main responsibilities now is to give presentations to current and potential clients.

Lynn's purpose is to help people live healthier lives. She pursues her purpose by trying to live a healthy life herself and by encouraging her family to eat well, stay active, and get enough sleep. She feels fortunate to work for a company that develops medical technology to improve the lives of people with health problems. She has had the opportunity to see the impact of the work her company does when she visits clients to give presentations. Keeping that in mind makes it easier to get through some of the more routine tasks of her job.

Part 4

What Matters Most

· ·

"Treasure your relationships,
not your possessions."

—Anthony J. D'Angelo

WHILE HAPPINESS AND MEANING are distinct constructs, they are correlated. Because of this, some of the strategies that I addressed in Parts 2 and 3 contribute to both dimensions of well-being. For example, in addition to increasing positive emotions, hope also gives us a sense of meaning by connecting our actions in the present with future goals. Using our strengths not only infuses us with meaning, but it also makes us happy. Aligning our behavior with our values makes us feel good, in addition to contributing to our sense that we are living authentic, meaningful lives.

One factor is equally important, perhaps even necessary, for both the feeling-good and the doing-good dimensions of well-being: our relationships. People who are thriving invest time and energy to improve the relationships they already have, as well as to make new connections. In chapter 9, I explain why relationships are so beneficial and discuss the importance of making an effort to spend time with people. Chapter 10 focuses on how you can build high-quality connections by engaging in positive interactions, showing appreciation, establishing trust, and being generous without over-giving.

9

Connect With Others

- -

"The best portion of your life will be the small, nameless moments you spend smiling with someone who matters to you."

—Ritu Ghatourey

IN HIS 2014 COMMENCEMENT speech at the University of Pennsylvania, singer John Legend said:

> *The key to success, the key to happiness, is opening your mind and your heart to love . . . It's about finding and keeping the best relationships possible with the people around you. It's about immersing yourself in your friendships and your family. It's about being there for the people you care about, and knowing that they'll be there for you.*

Human beings have a fundamental need to belong, to be an accepted member of a social group. Our need to form and maintain strong, stable relationships is a basic source of human motivation. The need to belong has two main features.[1] First is the need for frequent, positive interactions. These interactions make us happy.

The second is to perceive that we have an interpersonal bond with others that will endure over time. Having stable relationships contributes to our sense of meaning in life.

Thus, our relationships have an especially significant impact on our well-being because they influence both the feeling-good and the doing-good dimensions, increasing our joy and our life satisfaction. Relationships that serve to satisfy our own needs make us happy, while our contribution to the welfare of others increases our sense of meaning.[2]

A study at Harvard tracked 268 male undergrads for 75 years, starting in 1938, in order to discover the secrets to a fulfilling life. George Vaillant led the research for more than 30 years, and he published a summary of the findings in a book entitled *Triumphs of Experience: The Men of the Harvard Grant Study*.[3] Vaillant concluded that the warmth of people's relationships has the most significant impact on human flourishing. "The only thing that really matters in life are your relationships to other people," he said.

Martin Seligman and another prominent researcher in positive psychology, Ed Diener, surveyed over 200 students and found that the single factor that distinguished the very happiest students from everyone else was they all had close, meaningful connections with others.[4] Another study found that people who have at least three or four close friendships are happier, healthier, and more engaged.[5]

Relationships increase our positive emotions in a number of ways. They make us feel safe and can be a source of emotional support. When we face difficulties, one of the best coping mechanisms we have is to be able to share our problem with someone who cares. Having someone who will listen to us, reassure us, and help us think of solutions to our problem increases our positive emotions.

In addition to contributing to our happiness, people are also one of the main sources of meaning in life. Michael Steger and his colleagues gave digital cameras to college students and asked them to take pictures of what made their lives meaningful. They then asked the students to describe the pictures they took and explain how they contributed to life's meaning. Almost 90 percent of the students explicitly mentioned a relationship.[6]

During his imprisonment in a Nazi concentration camp, Viktor Frankl noted how fellow prisoners used their connections with others to endure. He believed that "a man who becomes conscious of the responsibility he bears toward a human being who affectionately waits for him . . . will never be able to throw away his life."[7] Roy Baumeister and his colleagues found that people who were asked to think about their social relationships subsequently reported higher levels of perceived meaning.[8] Becoming a parent may reduce our happiness because caring for children can be stressful, but it provides a substantial source of meaning in our lives.[9]

Our relationships impact our physical health and longevity, too. Individuals who enjoy high levels of social support have lower levels of stress and anxiety, stay healthier, and live longer. Another long-term study at Harvard, tracking 238,000 nurses since 1976, found that the more friends women have, the less likely they are to develop physical impairments as they age and the more likely they are to lead a joyful life.[10] In a different study, a group of researchers interested in how relationships affect physical health made small cuts on the arms of 12 married couples. The wounds of the couples who rated their marriages as positive healed twice as fast as the wounds of couples who reported higher levels of hostility in their relationship.[11] Positive relationships have also been found to increase resistance to upper respiratory infections and to boost the body's ability to fight off cancer.[12]

Researchers at Tel Aviv University were interested in isolating the factors that impact longevity. In 1988, they identified 820 healthy employees and tracked their health for the next 20 years.

During that period, 53 of the participants in the study died. The researchers determined that the risk of mortality was two times higher for those with low levels of social support.[13] At Duke University Medical Center, researchers studied patients with heart disease to explore the impact of relationships on health. Over a four-year span, people in the study with fewer than four friends were more than twice as likely to die from heart disease as those who had at least four friends.[14]

Barbara Fredrickson is a psychologist at the University of North Carolina in Chapel Hill where she directs the Positive Emotions and Psychophysiology Lab. In addition to her groundbreaking work in positive emotions, she has done fascinating research to understand the ways in which social connections affect our health. In her book *Love 2.0: Finding Happiness and Health in Moments of Connection*, Fredrickson explains how positive social encounters raise our oxytocin levels. Oxytocin has been called the "cuddle hormone" because it promotes caring behaviors, causing us to be more attuned to people and more open to emotional exchanges.[15]

Oxytocin protects the heart against the dangers of stress by lowering stress-induced increases in heart rate and blood pressure. It also reduces levels of the stress hormone cortisol in our bodies. So we experience significant health benefits as a result of the increased levels of oxytocin in our bodies that occur when we connect with others. Interestingly, Fredrickson found positive benefits of connecting with people we don't even know. A shared smile or short exchange with the person next to you in the grocery line is enough to trigger the release of oxytocin.[16]

There is so much research showing the impact of relationships on our well-being that positive psychologists have concluded that good social relationships don't just contribute to our well-being, but they are, in fact, necessary for it. Having a strong social network is vital in order to thrive.

You may feel like you are too busy to nurture your relationships. It does take time and effort to connect with others, but the benefits are worth it. How you choose to spend your time directly affects your well-being. People who are thriving recognize the value of close social ties and make an effort to spend time with others and to nurture their relationships.

Spend Time With Family and Friends

Robert Putnam is a Harvard professor who advises presidents and world leaders on issues of public policy. He studies topics as diverse as religion, immigration, class disparities, and social cohesion. In his book *Bowling Alone: The Collapse and Revival of American Community*, Putnam discusses how Americans have become increasingly disconnected. His research shows that we socialize with our family less often, meet with friends less frequently, know our neighbors less, and belong to fewer organizations. Putnam attributes these changes to technology, suburban sprawl, evolving values, and dual-career families.

Technology is causing us to become more connected electronically, yet more disconnected personally. Extreme work hours combined with long commutes and overscheduled kids makes it hard to find time in our packed schedules to connect with friends. It is easy to lose touch with people as our lives become more hectic. That's why you need to make staying in touch with friends a priority. It can be harder to get together once you have children or accept a job with more responsibility, but finding ways to stay connected is important for your well-being. Plan ahead to schedule a night out from time to time or a lunch or a weekend away to visit your college friends. For friends you have trouble seeing, a phone call can help you stay in touch.

Getting together with family can also take a lot of work. Often it requires travel, which involves planning and spending money, in addition to finding the time to get away. As I recounted earlier, when my husband and I were newlyweds, we moved to Spain to start our careers. My parents live in Alabama, and they were worried that they would never see us. This became an even greater concern when their first grandchild was born in Madrid. But we promised them from the start that family was a priority for us, and we made good on that promise by traveling back to the States to spend Christmas and summer holidays in Alabama.

At the beginning, we didn't have much money, but traveling to see family was how we spent the money we did have. We had a little more money when our children were born, but I promise you there is no amount of money that could make flying overseas with babies easy. That still didn't stop us. We had some really long, difficult trips between Spain and Alabama when our children were young (not to mention trying to get Christmas presents back and forth!), but each and every trip was worth it to stay connected to my family and to see the bond between my parents and children strengthen.

Build Relationships With Co-workers

Given that many of us spend as much time at work as we do anywhere else, relationships at work matter a great deal. Having positive relationships with colleagues can reduce our stress and increase our productivity. Employees who have a best friend at work are seven times more likely to be highly engaged than those who don't.[17] They are happier and, because positive emotions enhance both motivation and effectiveness, they have higher levels of performance.[18] People who have three or four close friendships at work are nearly 50 percent more satisfied with their company and are significantly more satisfied with their lives in general.[19] Do you have close friends at work?

Having friends at work gives us access to knowledge and information that can help us do our jobs better. Working with friends leads to greater collaboration and less conflict. People are more willing to go out of their way to help friends accomplish their tasks. How has one of your colleagues helped you out?

Friends can also help us cope with difficulties and bounce back quicker when we face challenges. When we work with people we feel close to it gives us a sense of security, so we are more willing to take risks and think creatively. Supportive relationships encourage us to go outside of our comfort zone, which leads to growth. Working with people we like energizes us and brings out our best ideas. Whom do you regularly check in with when you are at work?

I experienced the importance of having friends at work when I was trying to get tenure at the university in Madrid. My children were very young, which made the situation even more stressful. Many times I felt like throwing in the towel. But, fortunately, a few other women in my department were also trying to juggle raising small children with the demands of a tenure-track position. They would stop by my office and invite me to join them for coffee or to have lunch together. I often protested that I had too much work to do, but they always insisted. I ended up making some really good friends. Spending time with other women who were facing similar challenges significantly reduced my stress level. Their support was crucial at a time when it would have been very easy for me to give up. We encouraged each other to keep going and were even able to laugh at some of the situations in which we found ourselves.

Look for opportunities to form closer relationships at work. Make a point to spend time with people. Stop by the break room where people are hanging out. Have coffee with a friend or invite someone new to join you for lunch. When you feel stressed and under time pressure you will most likely want to eat lunch alone at your desk. Don't! Socializing will help to reduce your stress and, as a result, you will be much more effective when you go back to finish up your work.

Get to know people even better by getting together with co-workers outside of the office. Have them over for dinner, meet to have a picnic in the park with your families, go to a baseball game. What have you done to foster relationships with your colleagues? It isn't necessary to become friends with everyone, but nurturing a few good friendships at work will help you to thrive.

Mentors, or better yet sponsors, are especially important work relationships. A mentor is someone who shows you the ropes and gives you advice. Sponsorship goes beyond giving feedback and advice. Sponsors use their influence to advocate for someone, helping them to get a promotion or making sure they get visible stretch assignments. Mentoring helps people succeed at work; however, sponsoring is more directly linked to getting promoted.[20]

While women and men are equally likely to have mentors, men are more likely to have sponsors. Yet sponsorship is probably more crucial for advancing women's careers. Research shows that men typically judge their own performance to be better than it actually is, while women are more likely to judge their performance as worse than it really is.[21] Because we underestimate our capabilities, women are less likely to reach for opportunities than men. Men ask for challenging assignments or promotions, while women hang back, worried that they don't have the skills needed. Women need sponsors who will push them to do things they may not think they can do.

I had a wonderful sponsor as I began my career as a tenure-track professor. Isabel Gutiérrez was the director of the department when I was hired. She was in a position to be able to give me stretch assignments that would help me to grow, and she did just that. She appointed me to leadership positions within the department soon after I arrived. A few years later, she assigned me to teach a grad-uate-level class in research methods, knowing I could do it despite my own doubts. Then she appointed me to be the director of our department's new PhD program. Isabel saw what I was capable of and she sponsored me by putting me in positions that allowed me to grow and advance in my career.

Sponsorship is best achieved by building a close relationship with someone well placed in your organization. It should be a professional relationship where both sides feel a connection. Rather than asking someone directly to be your sponsor, look for situations where you will have a chance to interact with more senior members of your organization. Engage them in conversation so that they become aware of your strengths and interests. Look for specific opportunities to seek their knowledge or advice and let them know how much you appreciate their help. They will choose to sponsor you after getting to know you and becoming aware of your talents and potential.[22]

Establishing relationships with other professionals outside of your company is also valuable. Networking is a great way to expand your circle of social connections. People often dislike networking because they think it is about passing out business cards and asking people to help them find a job. Ideally, networking should be about creating and nurturing relationships. It may be the case that a connection you make through networking turns out to be useful to you in the future, but the immediate goal should be simply to create new relationships.

Look for ways to meet new people with whom you might have something in common. Join industry associations, volunteer for a cause that matters to you, take cooking classes, join a gym, or sign up for a book club. There are many groups for people with common interests (and common struggles!), such as working mothers, single working mothers, parents of teenagers, female lawyers, female executives, Latina professionals, and African American business women, among others.

Think of the ways you are currently networking. How have you benefited from these networks? What have you contributed to networks? What are two or three other networking environments that you could explore over the next few months?

What You Can Do:

- Make an effort to stay in touch with **family and friends**.

- Become friends with some of your **co-workers**.

- Build a diverse **network** of social connections.

10

Strengthen Your Relationships

. . . .

"Relationships create the fabric of our lives. They are the fibers that weave all things together."

—Eden Froust

CONNECTING WITH OTHERS IS important, but your happiness depends more on the strength of your relationships than on the number of your social connections. Every interaction you have is an opportunity to engage in a high-quality connection, which can lead to a positive spiral of mutual respect and positive regard.[1] The best way to nurture your relationships is to focus on building high-quality connections using positive interactions, appreciation, trust, and generosity.

Engage in Positive Interactions

"Good words are worth much, and cost little."

—George Herbert

Our natural tendency, because of our negativity bias discussed in chapter 2, is to pay more attention to what is going wrong than what is going right. A Gallup poll asked parents what they would focus on if their children brought home the following grades: two As, one C, and one F. The vast majority of parents in multiple countries said they would focus their attention on the F.[2] Managers typically focus on performance problems at work, as well.

While this makes it more likely that we notice potential threats, it can also mean that many of our interactions have a negative focus, which can undermine relationships. Negativity is much more powerful than positivity, negative emotions are felt more intensely and are remembered more readily; therefore, we need more positive than negative interactions to develop high-quality connections.

John Gottman is internationally known for his research over the past 40 years on marriage. He co-founded the Gottman Institute at the University of Washington, where he has conducted much of his work on couples' interactions. In one of his often-cited studies, he videotaped 15-minute conversations between husbands and wives. He analyzed the videotapes by counting the number of positive and negative interactions. Based on the ratio of positive-to-negative interactions, he predicted whether each couple would stay together or divorce. Ten years later, Gottman checked back with the couples to test his predictions. He had predicted which couples would stay together with 94 percent accuracy. Gottman concluded that a five-to-one ratio of positive-to-negative statements was necessary for a successful marriage.[3]

Clear benefits are associated with positive interactions, both for your personal relationships and for your success at work. So it is in your best interest to try to keep your interactions with others positive. Use supportive, affirmative language as often as you can. Give more compliments and limit your criticism. Don't nag. Look for what is good and mention that instead. Respond to people when they initiate a conversation. Ask to hear more and then listen with empathy. It takes a conscious effort to keep the balance of your interactions with others positive, but the effort can greatly enhance the quality of your relationships.

It can be easier to stay positive in a conversation when you focus on what you like about the person with whom you are interacting. Relationships are enhanced when you look for the good in others and keep their strengths in mind. Before you meet with people, think about their positive attributes. Then make a point to highlight one of them at the beginning of your conversation. If you start off on a positive note by expressing appreciation, people will feel validated and will be more likely to engage in conversation and to listen to what you have to say. The result will be a more open conversation with more sharing of information.

In his book *The Compound Effect: Jumpstart Your Income, Your Life, Your Success*, Darren Hardy tells a great story about the Thanks Giving journal he made for his wife.[4] For an entire year he secretly wrote one thing in his journal each day that he appreciated about his wife. He gave the finished journal to her on Thanksgiving. She said it was the best gift he had ever given her, although he claims that he was even more affected by the gift. By consciously looking for all the things that were good about his wife, he fell in love with her all over again, and his appreciation and gratitude for her changed his behavior toward her, which ultimately improved their marriage.

Interestingly, the way you respond to someone when good news is shared can be more important than how you respond during difficult times.[5] Active constructive responding is the best way to strengthen relationships by showing that you care about what someone has to say. You can do this by responding enthusiastically and showing genuine interest by asking for more details.

Contrast this with other ways of responding that show a lack of respect either actively, by responding negatively to what has been said, or passively, by failing to show interest. With active destructive responding, you acknowledge what the other person has said, but then add something negative. Imagine someone telling you he or she was just chosen to join the company's strategic planning committee and you say, "Wow, that is going to take up a lot of your time. I sure hope your family life doesn't suffer."

Passive constructive responding is giving a less than enthusiastic response, like "that's great," and then continuing on our way or talking about something else; whereas passive destructive responding is saying something completely unrelated to what we were just told. We basically ignore what the person has told us by changing the subject.[6]

I must admit that I am guilty at times of responding in not-so-constructive ways. I don't do it on purpose, but let's face it, I have so many other things to think about that I often just don't feel like I have the time to stop and ask to hear more. Sound familiar? Sometimes a little jealousy might lead us to say something negative to our colleague who was chosen for the strategic planning committee. Whatever the reason, each time we fail to respond in an active constructive way, we've lost an opportunity to connect with someone and show we really care about his or her happiness.

When interacting with people we don't know, compassion comes more easily if we start by assuming that people are good. They want the same things we do: to be to be safe from harm, to be healthy, to be loved, to be happy. They deserve respect and appreciate kindness.

Last summer, our family was on a plane and there was a child screaming somewhere behind us the whole flight. Later, when we were in line at customs, I heard the crying again and was surprised to see that it was a boy at least six years old with his mother. I commented to my children that I couldn't believe how old he was. I know it can be hard to keep a two year old from crying, but a six year old should know better. My daughter looked at me and said, "Mom, you don't know what he might be going through. Maybe his father just died, or he is in a lot of pain." She was right. I shouldn't have judged him. It reminded me of the title of *Good Morning America* co-anchor Robin Roberts' book *Everybody's Got Something*. We often don't know what is going on in other people's lives. Remembering this makes it easier to treat everyone with compassion and kindness.

Show Appreciation

"Appreciation can make a day, even change a life. Your willingness to put it into words is all that is necessary."

—Margaret Cousins

When people feel appreciated, connections are strengthened. Feeling appreciated is one of our strongest human needs. In her commencement speech at Harvard in May 2013, Oprah Winfrey remarked that one thing everyone she had interviewed over 25 years had in common was that when the interview was over, each asked, "How did I do? Was that okay?" Everyone—from business moguls, to heads of state, to entertainers, to criminals—wanted to be validated.

A good way to show appreciation is by demonstrating an interest in learning more about people. Be curious about those around you; inquire about their families, their hobbies, and their stories. The more you learn about people, the more likely you will find something you have in common; discovering similarities with someone else tends to strengthen your relationship. At work, make a point of having conversations with different colleagues; if they mention something you have in common, point it out.

Giving others your undivided attention makes them feel appreciated. When you talk to people, really listen to what they say. This shows that you are genuinely interested in them, that you respect their ideas and value their opinions. Being a good listener isn't easy. It requires setting aside whatever it is you are doing and really focusing on what the person is saying. Sherry Turkle, director of the MIT Initiative on Technology and Self, has found that just having a cell phone on the table when you are talking to someone changes the nature of the conversation, keeping it more superficial.[7]

Your body language is an important cue that you are listening. Leaning forward and making eye contact express interest and a desire to listen. Stay present in the conversation, trying not to let your mind wander or start formulating your response while someone is still talking. When the speaker finishes, pause before you respond. As my friend Kellye says, "Listen to the silence at the end of people's sentences." Pausing shows that you believe that the person has something to say that is worth waiting for. It also gives you a moment to prepare a mindful response. Becoming a good listener requires a conscious effort and lots of practice. I still work at it every day.

Other keys to active listening include paraphrasing and asking questions. Paraphrasing, or restating what you heard in your own words, is an effective way to let the speaker know that you understand what he or she said. It also gives the person a chance to clear up any potential misunderstandings. Following up with questions shows you are interested in hearing more.

The most obvious, yet remarkably underused, way to show appreciation is by saying "thank you." In chapter 4, I noted the very small percentage of people who express gratitude. At times we may be thankful for someone but feel shy or embarrassed about expressing our thanks. Sometimes we are too busy to stop and say "thank you." On other occasions, we simply take for granted what someone has done, so it doesn't occur to us to express our appreciation.

Saying "thank you" not only makes you and the person you thanked feel good, it can encourage helpful behaviors in the future. Adam Grant conducted a study with Francesca Gino to determine whether or not thanking people would motivate them to offer more help. They asked 69 students to provide feedback on a fellow student's job application cover letter. After the students sent their feedback, they received another email asking for help with a second cover letter. Half of the follow-up emails expressed gratitude for the assistance the students had provided; the other half did not. Sixty-six percent of the students who received the thank-you email helped with the second letter; only 32 percent of those who were not thanked offered additional help.[8]

In my family, expressing appreciation is a much better way to get help around the house than nagging. I make a point of noticing the good things they do and thank them for it. At first I thought, why should I thank my children for unloading the dishwasher? That's one of the household jobs they are expected to do. Nevertheless, I still appreciate it when they do it and saying "thank you" makes them feel good, so they are more likely to do it the next time without having to be reminded. Nagging makes people not want to be around you. Showing appreciation does just the opposite.

There is no better way to make people feel appreciated than to tell them directly. When someone does something for you, take the time to let that person know how much you appreciate it.

Establish Trust

"To be trusted is a greater compliment than being loved."

—George MacDonald

Positive relationships are built on trust. You can strengthen your relationships both by letting others feel that they can trust you and by showing that you trust them.

Be Trustworthy

Research on trust has found that people are perceived to be trustworthy when they act with integrity, dependability, and benevolence.[9] People with integrity are honest and truthful. Their decisions are guided by their values. This leads to a consistency between their beliefs and their behavior so they can be trusted to act in ways that are aligned with their values. Sometimes being honest is difficult because telling the truth might hurt someone's feelings; be sensitive and choose your words carefully, but tell the truth.

Dependable people can be counted on because they are responsible, consistent in their behavior, and use good judgment. We trust people who are dependable because we know we can rely on them. When we ask them to do something, we don't have to worry whether or not it will get done. We can trust them to do what they say they will do because they keep their promises.

Don't confuse being dependable with always agreeing when someone asks for help. It is actually just the opposite. Being dependable means keeping your commitments, which requires that you be especially careful not to over commit. If you aren't sure you will be able to do something, say "no." Don't agree to a request too quickly; take some time to think about whether or not you will be able to keep the commitment.

When you accept a commitment, write it down and make sure to find time to fulfill it. Plan how and when you will accomplish what you've promised. Write the deadline in your calendar and list the steps you need to take to complete the task. Once you've committed to something, do all that you can to follow through. Trust is built over time by keeping your promises. Tim Sanders, the former Yahoo! executive turned author, writes, "keep your promises because of who *you* are, not because of who *they* are."[10]

Because I'm a people pleaser, saying "no" has always been hard for me. I want to say "yes" when I'm asked for my help because I don't want to disappoint someone. But I have learned over many years of stressing myself out by putting too much on my plate that I must be very careful when making commitments. Choosing your commitments wisely builds close, trusting relationships by showing people that they can count on you.

Benevolence is a disposition to do good; to act kindly to others. Benevolent individuals are trusted because they provide others with a sense of security. People are more likely to trust someone who they believe cares about their best interest, someone who will share in their joys and commiserate with their troubles. Find ways to let family, friends, and co-workers know that you care about them—send birthday cards, call them when you know they are going through a difficult time, or take them out to dinner to celebrate a success.

Trust Others

It is also important in relationships to let people know that you trust them. This can be especially difficult, because in order to trust someone we have to be willing to be vulnerable. Vulnerability is when you risk getting emotionally hurt by being open and honest. According to Brené Brown, it is the core of meaningful human experiences. Brown is a professor at the University of Houston Graduate College of Social Work. Her 2010 TED Talk on the power of vulnerability is one of the most viewed TED Talks throughout the world. In her book *Daring Greatly: How the Courage to Be Vulnerable Transforms the Way We Live, Love, Parent, and Lead*, Brown discusses how embracing vulnerability is the key to truly connecting with others in order to live wholeheartedly.[11]

She explains that developing close relationships requires trusting others enough to be vulnerable. Most of us are afraid of letting people see who we really are. We worry that we're not good enough and fear exposing ourselves to the judgment of others. Vulnerability is about accepting that we aren't perfect and being willing to expose our imperfections.

More often than not, people appreciate when we are honest about what we do and don't know. Companies recognize the value of having employees who are willing to admit they don't know something. One company that provides information technology services actually includes questions about bogus software in the hiring interview in order to test candidates' willingness to be open and honest.

When we share information about ourselves, we demonstrate that we are willing to trust the other person with this information. Being vulnerable requires authenticity, courage, and self-compassion.[12] You need to be willing to let go of who you think you should be in order to be who you are. The willingness to be your true self, regardless of what other people think, is the first step. It takes courage to tell the story of who you really are and admit you aren't perfect, to say "I need help" or "I made a mistake" or "I want to go back to work, but don't know how."

The courage to be authentic is easier when you have self-compassion. Self-compassion means being supportive and sympathetic toward yourself when you notice personal shortcomings; having tolerance and understanding when you make mistakes or fail at something. It can be easier to have compassion for yourself if you remember that life's challenges and failures are part of being human. Nobody is perfect. Those smiling pictures you see on Facebook do not represent the whole picture. Everyone has weaknesses and personal failures. So don't be so hard on yourself.[13]

"You yourself, as much as anybody in the entire universe, deserve your love and affection."

—Buddha

Building close relationships requires that you open yourself up to others. Practicing self-compassion and accepting your own imperfections can help you embrace vulnerability and live wholeheartedly. Putting yourself out there means you have a much greater risk of feeling hurt. But nothing hurts as badly as living a life without the courage to let others know who you really are.[14]

Be Generous

"Those who bring sunshine to the lives of others cannot keep it from themselves."

—James M. Barrie

Generosity is important for strengthening relationships. It is giving without expecting anything in return. When we give freely of our time and emotional energy, others know we care about them. The University of Virginia's National Marriage Project looked at the role of generosity in the marriages of 2,870 men and women. Results showed that couples who reported a high amount of generosity in their relationship were 32 percent more likely to rate their marriage as "very happy."[15]

Giving helps us build close relationships with others. It also boosts our positive emotions. We get a rush of positive feelings when we help others. Cami Walker is an excellent example of how practicing acts of kindness can be good for you. At the age of 35, Walker was diagnosed with multiple sclerosis, a neurological condition that can make it difficult to walk or live a normal life. She became depressed, and, at a particularly low point, she decided to follow the advice of a friend and spiritual mentor to give something away each day for 29 days. Walker noticed that the more she gave away, the better she felt. Her health and her happiness both improved. She was so transformed by her giving experience that she wrote a book, *29 Gifts: How a Month of Giving Can Change Your Life*. Thousands of people around the world have now taken the 29-Day Giving Challenge.[16]

Interestingly, a completely unrelated study of women who had multiple sclerosis and volunteered as peer supporters for other women with the condition showed similar results. The benefits of the program, including increased satisfaction, self-efficacy, and feelings of mastery, were seven times greater for the volunteers than for the patients they supported.[17]

Several reasons explain why being generous increases your positivity. Helping others makes you feel good about yourself. Using your skills in acts of kindness can boost your self-confidence and give you a sense of accomplishment. Giving to others in need can help you appreciate your own good fortune. It gives you a sense of abundance. Generosity connects you with other people, those you are helping or other volunteers. These social interactions also contribute to higher levels of positivity. Finally, helping others can distract you from your own problems. You don't have as much time to worry about things in your own life if you are focused on someone else.

"When we give cheerfully and accept gratefully, everyone is blessed."

—Maya Angelou

Women are natural givers. We give to our children, to our spouses, to our friends, to our neighbors, and to our co-workers. All of this giving can enhance our relationships and boost our positivity; however, women need to be careful not to give too much.

Over-giving can lead to burnout. Sometimes we focus so much on giving to others that we don't take care of ourselves.

Wharton professor Adam Grant has written a book, *Give and Take: A Revolutionary Approach to Success*, about the benefits of helping others. In it he recognizes that giving can cause some people to experience burnout and suggests strategies that givers can use to avoid this.[18] Giving in these smart ways can lead to sustainable generosity.

Chunk Giving

Givers who "chunk" their giving by doing a lot of it at once are happier than those who spread their giving out over time. Doing five acts of kindness one day a week makes your giving more salient than doing the same five acts across five days.

Setting aside blocks of time to help others also lets you conserve time to attend to your own interests. It is important for givers to set limits on their availability. You can either establish quiet times when you are working and don't want to be interrupted or, alternatively, you can establish specific times that you are available for helping others.

As a college professor I always found office hours to be very helpful. I let students know at the beginning of each semester that I would be in my office available to answer their questions at certain times during the week. This made it easier for them because they knew if they dropped by my office at those times, I would be there. It also gave me a chance to schedule my help in a way that provided me with other moments of uninterrupted time to work. A similar schedule of "office hours" could be useful in a variety of workplaces.

Choose What to Give

People derive the greatest amount of satisfaction from giving when they help others out of a sense of enjoyment and purpose. Generosity is sustainable when givers are careful to choose causes that they feel are important and meaningful to them. Giving that is aligned with your strengths, interests, and values is more likely to be energizing. It gives you a sense of mastery and enjoyment.

When my children were younger, I wanted to volunteer at their school. The teachers had a list of volunteer opportunities that parents could sign up for at the beginning of the year. When my daughter started kindergarten, I signed up to help in the lunchroom. What was I thinking? Patience has never been a strength of mine, so handling a lunchroom full of screaming five-year-olds did not come naturally to me. I was a complete wreck by the time lunch was over. I realized that supervising lunch was not the best way for me to give of my time. Looking at the other volunteer opportunities, I saw that there was a need for helping students learn to write. So I traded lunch duty for writing support. Once a week, I helped out by walking around the classroom, teaching the children how to spell whatever it was they were trying to write about in their journals. I found such joy helping them learn new words and listening to their stories that my Friday morning volunteer time was something I looked forward to each week.

Seek Support

Givers also avoid burnout by soliciting the help of others. They understand the importance of social support for their own well-being and actively seek the assistance of others when they start to feel burned out.

Women often have trouble asking for what they need, because advocating for themselves goes against their self-image as a giver.[19] One way for us to become more assertive is to think about how what we want might also benefit others. A woman seeking support in terms of more flexibility at work might think about how much happier her family will be if she has greater flexibility. Shifting her frame of reference in order to see herself as advocating for her family will help her be assertive because she is doing it for them.

Generosity builds high-quality relationships. It also has a direct impact on our positive emotions. As the saying goes, "giving is its own reward." But giving in the wrong way can lead to burnout. Sustainable generosity allows you to reap the rewards of giving without the potential downsides.

Strong relationships bring you great joy and meaning. Building high-quality connections with others is a powerful strategy for thriving. Find time to connect with friends, family, and colleagues. Make an effort to have as many positive interactions as possible. Show others how much you appreciate them. Let people know you trust them and that they can trust you. Be generous, but be careful to give in ways that won't lead to burnout.

What You Can Do:

- Make an effort to **spend time** with others.

- Try to maximize the amount of **positive interactions** you have with others.

- Let people know you **appreciate** them.

- **Trust** others and act in ways that build their trust in you.

- Engage in **sustainable generosity**.

Let's return to Lynn one last time. What could she have done differently to strengthen her relationships? Imagine that instead of having lunch at her desk, Lynn takes a break from her work to have lunch with Susan. Susan is a senior executive in Lynn's firm, and they have become friends over the years. In fact, it was Susan who recommended Lynn for the promotion she received last year. Over lunch, Lynn mentions to Susan that she isn't sure she is the right person for a challenging assignment that her manager is encouraging her to accept. Susan assures her that she can do it. She laughs and points out that a man would jump at the chance without a moment of self-doubt. Lynn feels energized and upbeat when she returns to work.

She sees the invitation from Ann and responds, "Sounds great, I'm in!" She will need to adjust her schedule and make arrangements for the kids, but spending quality time with her girlfriends is worth the effort. That evening when Jeff rushes in, she smiles and tells him she is happy he made it home in time to eat with the family. After dinner, Lynn and Jeff go for a walk. He mentions his business trip, and they brainstorm ideas for how Lynn can manage things while he is gone.

Afterword:
From Struggling to Thriving

· ·

*"Nobody can go back and start
a new beginning, but anyone can start
today and make a new ending."*

—Maria Robinson

YOUR WELL-BEING DEPENDS ON two key elements: your happiness and your sense of meaning in life. Thriving comes from experiencing both pleasure and purpose. Please don't put this book down and move on to the next one without making a plan for how you are going to change your life for the better. Reading doesn't change your life. Your actions do. I know you are busy. We all are. Many of the suggestions in this book don't require much time or effort. Those that do are worth it. Your well-being is worth it.

"You have to participate relentlessly in the manifestation of your own blessings."

—Elizabeth Gilbert

Would you like to start with your happiness by increasing the amount of positive emotions that you experience? If so, you could practice being mindful. Slow down, stop multitasking, spend time outside, pause when you are emotionally triggered, or give meditation a try.

Another option is to be grateful. Pay attention to what is going well, count your blessings, express gratitude, and reframe situations to see them in a more positive light.

Maybe you'd like to be more hopeful. Visualize your ideal future, set goals, make a plan, and identify alternative paths for getting there. Pull out your victory log to remind yourself of your own successes and draw inspiration from others who have achieved their goals.

Don't stop at feeling good, though. Being happy is important for your well-being, but it's not enough. You also need to feel that your life has meaning; that you are doing good. Pick one of the exercises in chapter 6 to help you clarify your values and start making decisions that are based on your values. If you don't already know your life purpose, you might want to spend some time trying to discover your why.

Another strategy for increasing your sense of meaning is to identify and develop your strengths in order to fulfill your potential. Take a strengths assessment or solicit feedback from others. Find opportunities to use your strengths as often as possible.

Look for ways that you can make a positive difference. Remind yourself of the impact you are already making through your work. Keep the big picture in mind to avoid getting bogged down by mundane tasks. Also, think about ways in which you might change your job, either the tasks you do or the interactions you have with others, so that it gives you a greater sense of meaning.

Finally, remember that people matter most for your well-being because your relationships affect both the feeling-good and the doing-good dimensions. Spending time with people you like boosts your positive emotions. Having high-quality connections contributes to your sense of meaning in life.

Oftentimes, we fail to make positive changes because we have trouble getting started. Don't let this happen to you. Set an intention to create a happier, more meaningful life. Identify small steps that you can take to get the ball rolling. You don't need to do everything I've mentioned in this book in order to see a change in your well-being. Just pick one or two to get started. Small improvements can add up to big changes over time. Once you see the benefits of making positive change, you will likely want to try something more.

Look back at the results of the well-being assessment that you took in chapter 2. Was your Feeling Good or Doing Good score lower? If you are interested in increasing your positive emotions, consider how well you are currently doing as far as being mindful, grateful, and hopeful. Do you think you would benefit by making a change in one of these areas? If you'd rather start by increasing your sense of meaning in life, you could focus on living your values, developing your strengths, or making a positive impact. Perhaps you feel like strengthening your relationships is the best place for you to start. It could be a powerful way to boost both dimensions of your well-being.

Once you have decided where you want to focus, look at the tips suggested at the end of the corresponding chapter and choose one or two specific things that you will start doing to increase your well-being. Write them down. For each strategy you have written down, decide when and where you will do it. Schedule it on your calendar. Or better yet, try to turn it into a habit by choosing to do it at a particular time of day or at the same time that you consistently do something else. This will help you remember to do it and over time it will become automatic.

Are you going to start listing three good things that you experience each day? If you plan to do it before you go to sleep at night, put a small notebook and a pen by your bed as soon as you have a chance. Will you call your college roommate to reconnect? When? Why not send her a text right now to ask her if there is a good time for the two of you to talk? Perhaps you'd like to create a victory log. Schedule time on your calendar for when and where you will do it.

Like diet and fitness routines, different well-being strategies are more or less effective for different people. You need to try various activities to see which ones work best for you.[1] For example, I tried writing down three good things each night before going to bed but found it more frustrating than helpful. So instead, I count my blessings each morning when the kids head off to school. Saying goodbye to them is a cue that helps me to remember, and it's a great way to start my day off on a positive note.

Taking action and seeing results will boost your well-being. People typically feel that their best days are those when they make progress, while their worst days are when they have setbacks.[2] Consistent, meaningful progress can have a bigger impact on your motivation than big wins. Small changes create momentum, encouraging you to keep at it.

If you set a goal and then get off track, don't give up. People often abandon their goals when they slip up. If they eat something that isn't on their diet, they are more likely to continue to overindulge, telling themselves they have already ruined the day, so to hell with it. In fact, psychologists refer to this as the "what the hell" effect.[3]

Don't let a bad day or two cause you to throw in the towel. Let's say you decide that you are going to meditate for 20 minutes every day. There will be some days that you are too busy and just can't find the time. That's perfectly normal. Be kind to yourself. Accept the fact that you will have lapses. Don't beat yourself up when you do. People who have self-compassion are more likely to stick to their goals.

Focus on the progress you are making. Remind yourself that meditating just a few days a week is still more than you were doing before. Use your lapse as an opportunity to learn. Think about what you can do differently so that you will find time to meditate. Would it be better to do it first thing in the morning? Should you schedule it on your calendar? Make an adjustment and see how it goes.

Now is the time for you to stop reading and to start making progress. This book has provided you with knowledge regarding what can be done to improve your well-being, but nothing will change until you take action. Start today. It is time for you to thrive! I wish you the best of luck in your journey toward a more joyful, meaningful life.

Notes

· ·

Introduction

1. Brigid Schulte, *Overwhelmed: Work, Love, and Play When No One Has the Time* (New York: Sarah Crichton Books, 2014).
2. Betsey Stevenson and Justin Wolfers, "The Paradox of Declining Female Happiness," Working Paper (2009), http://www.nber.org/papers/w14969.pdf.
3. American Psychological Association, http://www.apa.org /news/press/releases/stress/2010/gender-stress.aspx.
4. "Care.com Survey Finds One in Four Working Moms Cry Alone at Least Once a Week," *Care.com*, accessed November 12, 2014, http://www.care.com/press-release-carecom-finds-1 -in-4-moms-cry-alone-once-a-week-p1186-q49877680.html.
5. "The Well-Being Project," http://www.cityofwellbeing .net/about/.

Chapter 1

1. Cathleen Benko and Anne Weisberg, *Mass Career Customization: Aligning the Workplace With Today's Nontraditional Workforce* (Boston: Harvard Business School Press, 2007).

2. Schulte, *op. cit.*

3. Fredrick Kunkle, "Daughters Provide Twice as Much Care for Aging Parents Than Sons Do, Study Finds," *Washington Post,* August 19, 2014, accessed December 10, 2014, http ://www.washingtonpost.com/national/health-science /daughters-provide-twice-as-much-care-for-aging-parents -than-sons-do-study-finds/2014/08/19/4b30cade-279b-11e4- 86ca-6f03cbd15c1a_story.html.

4. Elizabeth F. Cabrera, "Opting Out and Opting In: Understanding the Complexities of Women's Career Transitions," *Career Development International* 12:3 (2007): 218-237.

5. Claire Cain Miller and Liz Alderman, "Why U.S. Women Are Leaving Jobs Behind." *New York Times,* December 12, 2014, http://www.nytimes.com/2014/12/14/upshot /us-employment-women-not-working.html?smid=tw-share&_ r=1&abt=0002&abg=1.

6. Sheryl Sandberg, *Lean In: Women, Work, and the Will to Lead* (New York: Alfred A. Knopf, 2013).

7. Sylvia A. Hewlett and Carolyn B. Luce, "Extreme Jobs: The Dangerous Allure of the 70-Hour Workweek." *Harvard Business Review,* December 2006. hbr.org/2006/12/extreme- jobs-the-dangerous-allure-of-the-70-hour-workweek

8. Sandberg, *op. cit.*

9. Kristen P. Jones, Chad I. Peddie, Veronica L. Gilrane, Eden B. King, and Alexis L. Gray, "Not So Subtle: A Meta-Analytic Investigation of the Correlates of Subtle and Overt Discrimination," *Journal of Management* (2013): 1-26, doi: 10.1177/0149206313506466.

10. Debora L. Spar, *Wonder Women: Sex, Power, and the Quest for Perfection* (New York: Sarah Crichton Books, 2013).

11. Tanya Somanader, "Chart of the Week: The Persistent Gender Pay Gap," The White House, September 19, 2014, http://www. whitehouse.gov/blog/2014/09/19/chart-week -persistent-gender-pay-gap.

12. Sandberg, *op. cit.*
13. "2011 Research Financial Stress," *Financial Finesse Reports,* accessed December 11, 2014, http://www.financialfinesse .com/wp-content/uploads/2011/05/2011-Financial-Stress-Research.pdf.
14. Kim Parker and Wendy Wang, 2013. "Chapter 5: Americans' Time at Paid Work, Housework, Child Care, 1965 to 2011." Pew Research Center, March 14. www.pewsocialtrends. org/2013/03/14/chapter-5-americans-time-at-paid-work-housework-child-care-1965-to-2011/.
15. Joan C. Williams and Rachel Dempsey, *What Works for Women at Work: Four Patterns Working Women Need to Know* (New York: New York University Press, 2014).
16. Ellen Galinsky, Kerstin Aumann, and James T. Bond, "Times Are Changing: Gender and Generation at Work and at Home," *National Study of the Changing Workforce* (2008), accessed July 19, 2014, http://familiesandwork.org/site/research/reports/ Times_Are_Changing.pdf.
17. Joanna Barsh and Lareina Yee, "Unlocking the Full Potential of Women at Work," *McKinsey & Company Special Report* (2012), accessed July 23, 2014, http://www.mckinsey.com/ careers/women/~/media/Reports/Women/2012%20WSJ%20 Women%20in%20the%20Economy%20white%20paper%20 FINAL.ashx.
18. Spar, *op. cit.*
19. Cabrera, "Opting Out and Opting In: Understanding the Complexities of Women's Career Transitions."
20. Elizabeth F. Cabrera, "Protean Organizations: Reshaping Work and Careers to Retain Female Talent," *Career Development International* 14:2 (2009): 186-201.
21. Elizabeth F. Cabrera, "Using the Job Demands-Resources Model to Study Work-Family Conflict in Women," *The International Journal of Management and Business* 4:1 (2013): 112-124.

22. Cabrera, "Opting Out and Opting In: Understanding the Complexities of Women's Career Transitions."

Chapter 2

1. Carol Ryff, "Psychological Well-Being Revisited: Advances in the Science and Practice of Eudaimonia," *Psycotheraphy and Psychosomatics* 83 (2014): 10-28.
2. Joseph Ciarrochi, Todd B. Kashdan, and Russ Harris, "The Foundations of Flourishing," in *Mindfulness, Acceptance, and Positive Psychology: The Seven Foundations of Well-Being*, eds. Todd B. Kashdan and Joseph Ciarrochi (Oakland, CA: Context Press, 2013): 1-29.
3. Martin E. P. Seligman, *Flourish: A Visionary New Understanding of Happiness and Well-Being* (New York: Atria Books, 2011).
4. Jennifer Hecht, *The Happiness Myth: An Expose* (New York: HarperCollins, 2008).
5. Daniel Kahneman, *Thinking, Fast and Slow* (New York: Farrar, Straus and Giroux, 2013).
6. Sam Harris, "Thinking About Thinking: An Interview with Daniel Kahneman," The Blog, November 29, 2011, http://www.samharris.org/blog/item/thinking-about-thinking#sthash.vhQWISN3.dpuf.
7. Sonja Lyubomirsky, Laura King, and Ed Diener, "The Benefits of Frequent Positive Affect: Does Happiness Lead to Success?" *Psychological Bulletin* 131:6 (2005): 803-855.
8. Barbara L. Fredrickson and Christine Branigan, "Positive Emotions Broaden the Scope of Attention and Thought-Action Repertoires," *Cognition and Emotion* 19 (2005): 313-332.
9. Alice M. Isen, Andrew S. Rosenzweig, and Mark J. Young, "The Influence of Positive Affect on Clinical Problem Solving," *Medical Decision Making* 11 (1991): 221-227.
10. *Ibid.*
11. Deborah D. Danner, David A. Snowdon, and Wallace V. Friesen, "Positive Emotions in Early Life and Longevity: Findings from the Nun Study," *Journal of Personality and Social Psychology* 80 (2001): 804-813.

12. David Lykken, *Happiness: The Nature and Nurture of Joy and Contentment* (New York: St. Marten's Griffin, 1999).

13. *Ibid.*

14. Philip Brickman, Dan Coates, and Ronnie Janoff-Bulman, "Lottery Winners and Accident Victims: Is Happiness Relative?" *Journal of Personality and Social Psychology* 36 (1978): 917-927.

15. Laura M. Roberts, Gretchen Spreitzer, Jane Dutton, Robert Quinn, Emily Heaphy, and Brianna Barker, "How to Play to Your Strengths," *Harvard Business Review* 83:1 (January 2005): 75-80.

16. Rick Hanson, *Just One Thing: Developing a Buddha Brain One Simple Practice at a Time* (Oakland, CA: New Harbinger Publications, 2011).

17. José M. Soares, Adriana Sampaio, Luis Ferreria, Nadine Santos, Paulo Marques, Joana Palha, João Cerqueira, and Nuno Sousa, "Stress-Induced Changes in Human Decision-Making Are Reversible," *Translational Psychiatry* 2 (July 2012).

18. Hanson, *op. cit.*

19. Michael F. Steger, Joo Yeon Shin, Yerin Shim, and Arissa Fitch-Martin, "Is Meaning in Life a Flagship Indicator of Well-Being?" in *The Best Within Us: Positive Psychology Perspectives on Eudaimonia,* ed. Alan S. Waterman (Washington: American Psychological Association, 2013): 159-182.

20. Patricia A. Boyle, Lisa L. Barnes, Aron S. Buchman, and David A. Bennett, "Purpose in Life Is Associated With Mortality Among Community-Dwelling Older Persons," *Psychosomatic Medicine* 71 (2009): 574-579.

21. Roy F. Baumeister, Kathleen D. Vohs, Jennifer L. Aaker, and Emily N. Garbinsky, "Some Key Differences Between a Happy Life and a Meaningful Life," *The Journal of Positive Psychology* 8 (2013): 505-516.

22. Roy F. Baumeister, *Meanings of Life* (New York: Guilford, 1991).

23. Michael F. Steger, "Meaning in Life," in *Oxford Handbook of Positive Psychology,* eds. Shane J. Lopez and C. R. Snyder (New York: Oxford University Press, 2011): 667-688.

24. Kennon M. Sheldon and Andrew J. Elliot, "Goal Striving, Need Satisfaction, and Longitudinal Well-Being: The Self-Concordance Model," *Journal of Personality and Social Psychology* 76 (1999): 482-497.

25. Walter Isaacson, *Steve Jobs* (New York: Simon & Schuster, 2011).

26. Robert Biswas-Diener and Ben Dean, *Positive Psychology Coaching: Putting the Science of Happiness to Work for Your Clients* (Hoboken, NJ: John Wiley & Sons, 2007).

27. Barbara L. Fredrickson, Karen M. Grewen, Kimberly A. Coffey, Sara B. Algoe, Ann M. Firestine, Jesusa M. G. Arevalo, Jeffrey Ma, and Steven W. Cole, "A Functional Genomic Perspective on Human Well-Being," *Proceedings of the National Academy of Sciences* 110 (2013): 13684-13689.

Chapter 3

1. Jon Kabat-Zinn, *Wherever You Go, There You Are: Mindfulness Meditation in Everyday Life* (New York: Hyperion, 1994).

2. Mary Schmich, "Advice, Like Youth, Probably Just Wasted on the Young," *Chicago Tribune,* June 1, 1997.

3. Todd B. Kashdan and Robert Biswas-Diener, *The Upside of Your Dark Side: Why Being Your Whole Self—Not Just Your "Good" Self—Drives Success and Fulfillment* (New York: Hudson Street Press, 2014).

4. Viktor Frankl, *Man's Search for Meaning* (Boston: Beacon Press, 1946).

5. Gene Weingarten, "Pearls Before Breakfast: Can One of the Nation's Great Musicians Cut Through the Fog of a D.C. Rush Hour? Let's Find Out," *Washington Post Magazine,* accessed November 18, 2004, http://www.washingtonpost.com/lifestyle/magazine/pearls-before-breakfast-can-one-of-the-nations-great-musicians-cut-through-the-fog-of-a-dc-rush-hour-lets-find-out/2014/09/23/8a6d46da-4331-11e4-b47c-f5889e061e5f_story.html.

6. Elisha Goldstein, *The Now Effect: How a Mindful Moment Can Change the Rest of Your Life* (New York: Atria Books, 2013).

7. Joshua S. Rubinstein, David E. Meyer, and Jeffrey E. Evans, "Executive Control of Cognitive Processes in Task Switching," *Journal of Experimental Psychology: Human Perception and Performance* 27:4 (2001): 763-797.

8. David Rock, *Your Brain at Work: Strategies for Overcoming Distraction, Regaining Focus, and Working Smarter All Day Long* (New York: Harper Collins, 2009).

9. Karen Martin, *The Outstanding Organization: Generate Business Results by Eliminating Chaos and Building the Foundation for Everyday Excellence* (New York: McGraw-Hill, 2012).

10. Barbara Fredrickson, *Positivity: Top-Notch Research Reveals the 3 to 1 Ratio That Will Change Your Life* (New York: Three Rivers Press, 2009).

11. Chade-Meng Tan, *Search Inside Yourself: The Unexpected Path to Achieving Success, Happiness* (and World Peace) (New York: HarperOne, 2012).

Chapter 4

1. Jennifer Lockwood-Shabat, "Luncheon Remarks," *Washington Area Women's Foundation*, accessed November 18, 2014, http://thewomensfoundation.org/2014/jennifer-lockwood-shabats-luncheon-remarks/.

2. Robert A. Emmons and Michael E. McCullough, "Counting Blessings Versus Burdens: An Experimental Investigation of Gratitude and Subjective Well-Being in Daily Life," *Journal of Personality and Social Psychology* 84 (2003): 377-389.

3. Robert A. Emmons, "Acts of Gratitude in Organizations," in *Positive Organizational Scholarship: Foundations of a New Discipline*, eds. Kim S. Cameron, Jane E. Dutton, and Robert E. Quinn (San Francisco: Berrett-Koehler, 2003): 81-93.

4. Hanson, *op. cit.*

5. Robert Biswas-Diener, "Lessons on Happiness and Its Causes," Positive Acorn Blog, June 11, 2011, http://myemail.constantcontact.com/Happiness-and-its-Causes.html?soid=1102621930729&aid=SRVe9gAT2BQ.

6. Emiliana R. Simon-Thomas and Jeremy Adam Smith, "How Grateful Are Americans?" *Greater Good: The Science of a Meaningful Life*, January 10, 2013, http://greatergood.berkeley.edu/article/item/how_grateful_are_americans.

7. John Kralik, *365 Thank Yous: The Year a Simple Act of Daily Gratitude Changed My Life* (New York: Hyperion, 2010).

8. Tim Sanders, *Today We Are Rich: Harnessing the Power of Total Confidence* (Carol Stream, IL: Tyndale House Publishers, 2011).

Chapter 5

1. Elizabeth F. Cabrera, "The Six Essentials of Workplace Positivity," *People & Strategy* 35:1 (2012): 50-60.

2. Heidi G. Halvorson, *Succeed: How We Can Reach Our Goals* (New York: Plume, 2011).

3. Michelle C. Haynes and Madeline E. Heilman, "It Had to Be You (Not Me)!: Women's Attributional Rationalization of Their Contribution to Successful Joint Work Outcomes," *Personality & Social Psychology Bulletin* 39:7 (2013): 956-969.

4. Sandberg, *op. cit.*

5. "The Most Important Thing Is Hope: One Woman's Story of Recovering From Bipolar Disorder," *Brain & Behavior Research Foundation*, February 24, 2014, https://bbrfoundation.org/stories-of-recovery/the-most-important-thing-is-hope.

6. "About the Story Exchange," *The Story Exchange*, accessed November 7, 2014, http://thestoryexchange.org/about-us/.

Chapter 6

1. Michael F. Steger, Kelly Sheline, Leslie Merriman, Todd B. Kashdan, and Joseph Ciarrochi, "Using the Science of Meaning to Invigorate Values-Congruent, Purpose-Driven Action," in *Mindfulness, Acceptance, and Positive Psychology: The Seven Foundations of Well-Being*, eds. Todd B. Kashdan and Joseph Ciarrochi (Oakland, CA: Context Press, 2013), 240-266.

2. Michael Bungay Stanier, *Do More Great Work: Stop the Busywork, and Start the Work That Matters* (New York: Workman, 2010).

3. Steger, Sheline, Merriman, Kashdan, and Ciarrochi, *op. cit.*

4. Michele Roberts, "Flex Maven Allison O'Kelly," *Working Mother*, accessed September 15, 2014, http://www.workingmother.com/entrepreneur-mom/flex-maven-allison-okelly.

Chapter 7

1. Donald O. Clifton and James K. Harter, "Investing in Strengths," in *Positive Organizational Scholarship: Foundations of a New Discipline*, eds. Kim S. Cameron, Jane E. Dutton, and Robert E. Quinn (San Francisco: Berrett-Koehler, 2003): 111-121.

2. Robert Biswas-Diener, Todd B. Kashdan, and Gurpal Minhas, "A Dynamic Approach to Psychological Strength Development and Intervention," *The Journal of Positive Psychology* 6 (2011): 106-118.

3. Martin E. P. Seligman, *Authentic Happiness: Using the New Positive Psychology to Realize Your Potential for Lasting Fulfillment* (New York: Free Press, 2002).

4. Laura M. Roberts, Gretchen Spreitzer, Jane Dutton, Robert Quinn, Emily Heaphy, and Brianna Barker, "How to Play to Your Strengths," *Harvard Business Review* 83:1 (January 2005): 75-80.

5. "Job Crafting: Shaping Your Job to Fit You Better," Mind Tools, accessed October 23, 2014, http://www.mindtools.com/pages/article/newCDV_36.htm.

6. Carol F. Cohen and Vivian S. Rabin, *Back on the Career Track: A Guide for Stay-at-Home Moms Who Want to Return to Work* (New York: Warner Business Books, 2007).

Chapter 8

1. Steve Gladis and Beth Cabrera, "Purposeful Work: How to Find Your Next Job—One That Really Matters," *T+D* (February 2014): 64-65.

2. Stanier, *op. cit.*

3. Steger, Sheline, Merriman, Kashdan, and Ciarrochi, *op. cit.*

4. Gladis and Cabrera, *op. cit.*

5. "About EmpowHER," *EmpowHER,* accessed October 17, 2014, http://www.empowher.com/company.

6. Tony Schwartz and Christine Porath, "Why You Hate Work," *New York Times,* May 30, 2014, accessed October 15, 2014, http://www.nytimes.com/2014/06/01/opinion/sunday/why-you-hate-work.html?_r=2.

7. Amy Wrzesniewski, Clark McCauley, Paul Rozin, and Barry Schwartz, "Jobs, Careers, and Callings: People's Relations to Their Work," *Journal of Research in Personality* 31 (1997): 21-33.

8. Adam M. Grant, "The Significance of Task Significance: Job Performance Effects, Relational Mechanisms, and Boundary Conditions," *Journal of Applied Psychology* 93:1 (January 2008): 108-124.

9. Timo Vuori, Elina San, and Mari Kira, "Enthusiastic About a Job? Meaningfulness Making at Work" (Academy of Management Annual Meeting, Chicago, IL, August 7-11, 2009).

10. Adam Leipzig, "How to Know Your Life Purpose in 5 Minutes," accessed May 12, 2014, https://www.youtube.com/watch?v=vVsXO9brK7M.

11. Allison Glock, "How 'The Robin Hood of Interior Design' Changes Lives, One Makeover at a Time," *Oprah Magazine,* September 2014.

12. Justin M. Berg, Jane E. Dutton, and Amy Wrzesniewski, "Job Crafting and Meaningful Work," in *Purpose and Meaning in the Workplace,* eds. Bryan J. Dik, Zinta S. Byrne, and Michael F. Steger (Washington: American Psychological Association, 2013): 81-104.

13. Catherine Rampell, "U.S. Women on the Rise as Family Breadwinner," *New York Times*, May 29, 2013, accessed November 10, 2014, http://www.nytimes.com/2013/05/30/business/economy/women-as-family-breadwinner-on-the-rise-study-says.html.
14. "Park History," *Friends of Hanes Park*, accessed November 12, 2014, http://friendsofhanespark.org.

Chapter 9

1. Roy F. Baumeister and Mark R. Leary, "The Need to Belong: Desire for Interpersonal Attachment as a Fundamental Human Motivation," *Psychological Bulletin* 117:3 (1995).
2. Roy F. Baumeister, Kathleen D. Vohs, Jennifer L. Aaker, and Emily N. Garbinsky, "Some Key Differences Between a Happy Life and a Meaningful Life," *The Journal of Positive Psychology* 8 (2013): 505-516.
3. George E. Vaillant, *Triumphs of Experience: The Men of the Harvard Grant Study* (Cambridge, MA: Belknap Press, 2012).
4. Ed Diener and Martin E. P. Seligman, "Very Happy People," *Psychological Science* 13 (2002): 81-84.
5. Tom Rath and Jim Harter, *Wellbeing: The Five Essential Elements* (New York: Gallup Press, 2010).
6. Steger, Sheline, Merriman, Kashdan, and Ciarrochi, *op. cit.*
7. Frankl, *op. cit.*
8. Nathaniel M. Lambert, Tyler F. Stillman, Joshua A. Hicks, Shanmukh Vasant Kamble, Roy F. Baumeister, and Frank D. Fincham, "To Belong Is to Matter: Sense of Belonging Enhances Meaning in Life," *Personality and Social Psychology Bulletin* 39:11 (November 2013), 1418-1427.
9. Baumeister, Vohs, Aaker, and Garbinsky, *op. cit.*
10. Caroline Adams Miller and Michael B. Frisch, *Creating Your Best Life: The Ultimate Life List Guide* (New York: Sterling, 2009).

11. Janice K. Kiecolt-Glaser, Timothy J. Loving, Jeffrey R. Stowell, William B. Malarkey, Stanley Lemeshow, Stephanie L. Dickinson, and Ronald Glaser, "Hostile Marital Interactions, Proinflammatory Cytokine Production and Wound Healing," *Archives of General Psychiatry* 62:12 (2005): 1377-1384.

12. Kim Cameron, *Positive Leadership: Strategies for Extraordinary Performance* (San Francisco: Berrett-Koehler, 2012).

13. Arie Shirom, Sharon Toker, Yasmin Alkaly, Orit Jacobson, and Ran Balicer, "Work-Based Predictors of Mortality: A 20-Year Follow-Up of Healthy Employees," *Health Psychology* 30:3 (2011), 268-275.

14. Tom Rath, *Vital Friends: The People You Can't Afford to Live Without* (New York: Gallup Press, 2006).

15. Barbara Fredrickson, *Love 2.0: Finding Happiness and Health in Moments of Connection* (New York: Hudson Street Press, 2013).

16. *Ibid.*

17. Tom Rath and Donald O. Clifton, *How Full Is Your Bucket?* (New York: Gallup Press, 2004).

18. Elizabeth F. Cabrera, "The Six Essentials of Workplace Positivity," *People & Strategy* 35:1 (2012): 50-60.

19. Rath, *op. cit.*

20. Herminia Ibarra, Nancy M. Carter, and Christine Silva, "Why Men Still Get More Promotions Than Women," *Harvard Business Review* 88:9 (September 2010): 80-85.

21. D. Scott Lind, Stelios Rekkas, Viet L. Bui, Tony Lam, E. A. Beierle, and Edward M. Copeland, "Competency-Based Student Self-Assessment on a Surgery Rotation," *Journal of Surgical Research* 105:1 (2002), 31-34.

22. Sandberg, *op. cit.*

Chapter 10

1. Jane E. Dutton, *Energize Your Workplace: How to Create and Sustain High-Quality Connections at Work* (San Francisco: Jossey-Bass, 2003).

2. Rath and Clifton, *op. cit.*

3. John M. Gottman, *What Predicts Divorce? The Relationship Between Marital Processes and Marital Outcomes* (Hillsdale, NJ: Erlbaum, 1994).

4. Darren Hardy, *The Compound Effect* (New York: Vanguard Press, 2012).

5. Shelly L., Gable, Harry T. Reis, Evan R. Asher, and Emily A. Impett, "What Do You Do When Things Go Right?: The Intrapersonal and Interpersonal Benefits of Sharing Positive Events," *Journal of Personality and Social Psychology* 87:2 (2004): 228-245.

6. *Ibid.*

7. Sherry Turkle, *Alone Together: Why We Expect More From Technology and Less From Each Other* (New York: Basic Books, 2012).

8. Adam M. Grant and Francesca Gino, "A Little Thanks Goes a Long Way: Explaining Why Gratitude Expressions Motivate Prosocial Behavior," *Journal of Personality and Social Psychology* 98:6 (2010): 946-955.

9. John K. Rempel, John G. Holmes, and Mark P. Zanna, "Trust in Close Relationships," *Journal of Personality and Social Psychology* 49:1 (1985): 95-112.

10. Sanders, *op. cit.*

11. Brené Brown, *Daring Greatly: How the Courage to Be Vulnerable Transforms the Way We Live, Love, Parent, and Lead* (New York: Gotham, 2012).

12. *Ibid.*

13. Kristin D. Neff, "Self-Compassion: An Alternative Conceptualization of a Healthy Attitude Toward Oneself," *Self and Identity* 2 (2003): 85-102.

14. Brown, *ibid.*

15. W. Bradford Wilcox and Elizabeth Marquardt, eds., *The State of Our Unions: Marriage in America 2011* (Charlottesville, VA: The National Marriage Project, 2011), accessed September 8, 2014, http://nationalmarriageproject.org/wp-content/uploads /2012/05/Union_2011.pdf.

16. Cami Walker, *29 Gifts: How a Month of Giving Can Change Your Life* (Cambridge, MA: Da Capo Press, 2009).
17. Sonja Lyubomirsky, *The How of Happiness: A Scientific Approach to Getting the Life You Want* (New York: Penguin, 2007).
18. Adam M. Grant, *Give and Take: A Revolutionary Approach to Success* (New York: Viking, 2013).
19. Adam M. Grant, "In the Company of Givers and Takers," *Harvard Business Review* 91:4 (2013): 90-97.

Afterword

1. Lyubomirsky, *op. cit.*
2. Teresa Amabile and Steven Kramer, *The Progress Principle: Using Small Wins to Ignite Joy, Engagement, and Creativity at Work* (Boston: Harvard Business School Press, 2011).
3. Winona Cochran and Abraham Tesser, "The 'What the Hell' Effect: Some Effects of Goal Proximity and Goal Framing on Performance," in *Striving and Feeling: Interactions Among Goals, Affect, and Self-Regulation,* eds. Leonard L. Martin and Abraham Tesser (Hillsdale, NJ: Lawrence Erlbaum Associates, 1996), 99-120.

Further Reading

. . . .

Belkin, Lisa. "The Opt-Out Revolution," *New York Times Magazine*, October 26, 2003, 42.

Cabrera, Elizabeth F. "Fixing the Leaky Pipeline: Five Ways to Retain Female Talent," *People & Strategy* 32, no. 1 (2009): 40-45.

Fredrickson, Barbara L. 2009. *Positivity: Top-Notch Research Reveals the 3 to 1 Ratio That Will Change Your Life*. New York: Three Rivers Press.

Grant, Adam M. 2013. *Give and Take: A Revolutionary Approach to Success*. New York: Viking.

Ibarra, Herminia. 2003. *Working Identity: Unconventional Strategies for Reinventing Your Career*. Boston: Harvard Business School Press.

Lopez, Shane J. 2013. *Making Hope Happen: Create the Future You Want for Yourself and Others*. New York: Atria Books.

Lyubomirsky, Sonja. 2007. *The How of Happiness: A Scientific Approach to Getting the Life You Want*. New York: Penguin Press.

Rath, Tom, and Jim Harter. 2010. *Wellbeing: The Five Essential Elements*. New York: Gallup Press.

Schulte, Brigid. 2014. *Overwhelmed: Work, Love, and Play When No One Has the Time*. New York: Sarah Crichton Books.

Seligman, Martin E. P. 2002. *Authentic Happiness: Using the New Positive Psychology to Realize Your Potential for Lasting Fulfillment.* New York: Free Press.

———, 2011. *Flourish: A Visionary New Understanding of Happiness and Well-Being.* New York: Atria Books.

Spar, Debora L. 2013. *Wonder Women: Sex, Power, and the Quest for Perfection.* New York: Sarah Crichton Books.

Thornton, Mark. 2006. *Meditation in a New York Minute: Super Calm for the Super Busy.* Louisville, CO: Sounds True.

Williams, Joan C., and Rachel Dempsey. 2014. *What Works for Women at Work: Four Patterns Working Women Need to Know.* New York: New York University Press.

About the Author

· ·

ETH CABRERA IS AN organizational psychologist dedicated to helping individuals and organizations thrive. After receiving her doctorate from the Georgia Institute of Technology, she moved to Spain, where she was a professor of management at Universidad Carlos III de Madrid. She later taught and conducted research at Arizona State University and Thunderbird School of Global Management. Currently, Beth is a senior scholar at George Mason University's Center for the Advancement of Well-Being. She lives in Fairfax, Virginia, with her husband and their two children.

Index ·

· ·

A

action steps
  to achieve goals, 67–71
  to improve happiness,
    145–149
active listening, 134–136
active responses, constructive and
  destructive, 131–132
affirmative language, 130–131
alternatives, identifying after
  setbacks, 69–70, 75
American Psychological Association, viii, 19
Angelou, Maya, 1, 140
Ansari, Anousheh, 65–66, 69
Ansari X Prize, 65–66
anxiety, using to improve focus, 43
appreciation, showing of, 133–135,
  143
Aristotle, 104
assessments, to identify strengths,
  94–95
attentive listening, 47–48
*Authentic Happiness: Using the
  New Positive Psychology to
  Realize Your Potential for
  LastingFulfillment*
    (Seligman), 21
authenticity, modeling of, 83. *See
  also* values, living of
Awakenings Project, 72

B

Barnett, Margaret, 113
Barrie, James M., 139
Baumeister, Roy, 28-29, 31, 121
behavior, aligning with values,
  82–84, 88
Belkin, Lisa, 15
Bell, Joshua, 45
benevolence, trust and, 136. *See
  also* generosity
Biswas-Diener, Robert, 43
blessings, counting of, 59–60
body language, listening and, 134
*Bowling Alone: The Collapse and
  Revival of American Commu-
  nity* (Putnam), 123
brainstorming, of alternative plans,
  69–70
Brown, Brené, 137–138
Bryan, Daniela, 43
Buddha, 139

C

Care.com survey, ix
Centre for Applied Positive
  Psychology, 94–95
change, positive impact of making,
  112–115, 116
Chung, Alison, 73
chunk giving, 141–142
Churchill, Winston, 108
Ciarrochi, Joseph, 19–20